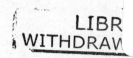

Loving Other People's Children

*An Essential Guide
for Step-parents*

DEBORAH FOWLER

VERMILION
LONDON

Published in 1992 by Vermilion
an imprint of Ebury Press
Random House UK Ltd
20 Vauxhall Bridge Road
London SW1V 2SA

British Library Cataloguing in Publication Data is available
from the British Library.

ISBN 0 09177386 5

Typeset in 11/12pt Garamond by
Hope Services (Abingdon) Ltd
Printed and bound in Great Britain by
Mackays of Chatham Plc, Kent

Contents

For Lorne, Innes, Russell and Murray – thanks
for putting up with me .

Acknowledgements

I have had a great deal of help and support in the writing of this book, but I particularly would like to thank:

Jane Allan of Oxfordshire Social Services
Relate for their invaluable help
Martin Berry, our family lawyer
Viola Niness, my patient secretary
My long-suffering family
and above all, of course, the parents,
step-parents and stepchildren who have contributed their own personal stories.

Introduction

Half the world's children are starving to death. Our senses are constantly reeling from shock at seeing images of suffering children the world over – in Africa, in Kurdistan, in the orphanages of Romania, in refugee camps around the world. At home the media fill our heads full of stories of sexual abuse, satanic rituals, snuff movies . . . every kind of child pornography. Against this background it is easy to write off the breakdown of a family as nothing more than a temporary hiccup in the life of a child. Yet in truth, the suffering inflicted on children caught up in parental divorce and separation is on a massive scale, and all the more damaging because, in so many instances, it is not fully understood or appreciated.

As a stepmother to four boys, I have a great deal of personal experience to draw on while writing about step-parenthood. My own daughter, too, has had to cope with her parents' marriage breaking up and the acquisition of a stepfather. Now she is a seventeen-year-old, and her views have proved invaluable. Indeed, in the preparation of this book I have called on the experience and advice of many step-parents, parents and children involved in the complexities of a stepfamily. The use of case histories I hope will make interesting and informative reading. Certainly, I believe that our pooled experiences have a great deal to offer in areas where textbook theory can be found wanting. I have also quite specifically drawn on the valuable professional expertise of such organisations as Relate (formerly the Marriage Guidance Council), Stepfamily and the social services of local authorities.

The main aim of this book is to try and lead step-parents and parents alike through the jumbled mass of emotions – their own and their children's – which are likely to surround the setting up of a stepfamily. I am in no position to preach, because I, too, have inadvertently caused my children pain by having a failed marriage. Having been through a fair number of family dramas, I have enormous sympathy for all step-parents and parents caught up in difficult situations. But I must admit that I cannot help standing on the side of the children. We all have choices. In this country, with the exception of minority cultures, marriages are not arranged. We alone decide whom we shall marry; and, with modern contraception and a realistic attitude to abortion, the decision to have a child should be just that – a decision, not an act of God. Children do not ask to be born into an ailing relationship, but they have to cope with the consequences. It is important that we do not lose sight of this fact, however difficult our children may be.

It is impossible to be the perfect parent, still more so the perfect step-parent, for the role is so infinitely variable and the rules far from clear-cut. Let us try to make sense of it all.

The Role of the Step-parent

Step-parents have had a pretty lousy press over the centuries. Stepmothers, of course, are traditionally wicked in all the best children's fairy stories, while in modern times it seems to be the stepfather who plays the central role in abuse cases – the man who refuses to accept another man's child. Set against this background, it is small wonder that the word 'step-parent' does not conjure up a very attractive image. Much of the problem seems to stem from the fact that the role is seen as a one-way affair. In other words, it is the duty of step-parents to care for their stepchildren; but there is no onus on the children to love or obey their step-parents, particularly when they have natural parents of their own. Indeed, the step-parent is almost expected to be mean, cruel and unloving.

My daughter, Lucy, was at a friend's house when he announced to the assembled company that his father was going to remarry. There were universal cries of horror and a rush of sympathy from everyone present. The poor unfortunate woman who was about to become the boy's stepmother was condemned before anyone had even met her. It was naturally assumed that she would be an unwelcome arrival in the boy's life – not helpful or loving.

Double standards

It is this double standard – the difference between what a step-parent is expected to give and what he or she actually receives – which causes much of the heartache in stepfamilies. The role is confused because there is no formula laid down for how a step-parent should behave, and expectations vary so hugely. You fall in love, you marry, you accept that with your new partner comes a package deal – his or her children by a previous marriage or relationship. So far, so good. It is only when the real business of living together starts that all too often you find you are married to a schizophrenic. You are the centre of your new partner's universe when his or her children are not around, but when they are, your partner's focus completely changes. Understandable – certainly; reasonable – possibly; but acceptable – no. The kind of behaviour your partner would not tolerate from any other living soul he or she accepts without a murmur from his or her children. After all, they have been traumatised – patience and understanding are required in unrealistic quantities, and surely it is perfectly natural that they should resent a new member of the family.

Outsiders

All too often, within weeks or even days of getting married step-parents begin to feel like outsiders. There are so many shared experiences from the former family of which they can never be a part, so many ways of doing things which are foreign to them. Talking to step-parents, this is something which crops up time and time again – the feeling of being an outsider looking in, the feeling of not being able to compete with what went before.

It is here that the real key to successful step-parenthood lies. It is no good trying to be something which you are not – the natural parent to your stepchildren. Even if the role you are taking on is a result of the child's natural parent having died, and even if that child is very young, it is still inadvisable to try and assume the role of full parent, at least not until you are invited to do so. Jane learned the hard way:

When Barry and I met, his daughters were seven and nine. Their mother had tragically died of cancer, three and a half years earlier, and Barry had been coping on his own with the help of his mother and a part-time house-keeper. I didn't make the classic mistake – in other words I didn't expect the girls to love me or to call me Mummy, and I didn't assume that I could simply march into their lives and take over where their mother left off.

None the less I did want to improve the quality of their life. Sometimes there was no one there when they came home from school. There was no real structure – each day was a bit haphazard, and although there was a lot of love around, the house had a sort of drab, neglected look about it – it was no longer really a home, more a lodging place.

I wanted to be a good wife to Barry and yes, stepmother to his children, so Barry and I agreed that I should give up my job and be at home full-time – it was what we both wanted. I was very careful not to change anything, at least not at once, but I was always there when the girls came home from school, with a smashing tea. I took an interest in what they were doing. I read them stories at bedtime and tucked them up. I bought them new clothes, and gradually began to do little things like make new curtains.

Everything I did for them they greeted with a cool, slightly sullen attitude. They were never rude, but nor were they appreciative or warm in any way. When I kissed them goodnight, they simply offered me their cheek and never kissed me back. When Barry and I were in the room together they tended to address all their remarks to him, never to me – quite literally as if I didn't exist. Barry thought I was being over-sensitive, but then men don't see things like that, do they?

The weeks turned into months, and nothing seemed to get better. I was becoming more and more depressed and it was starting to affect our marriage. Barry was entirely on the side of his girls – he seemed to think I should have limitless patience and compassion. Eventually, after lunch with a girlfriend one day, I made the decision to go back to work. It was the best thing I ever did.

Barry was appalled and so were the girls, but I told them I wasn't really needed too much at home. I said I loved them all dearly and would continue to look after them when I came back from work, but I needed a life of my own. It was fascinating – they tried everything to stop me. But I went ahead, and was lucky enough to find a vacancy at my old firm.

From the very first day the girls began to be more appreciative, warmer and friendlier. They began doing things for me – like making me a cup of tea when I got in from work. I couldn't believe the difference.

I talked it over with Barry, and he did admit that he could see how their behaviour had improved. So gradually I eased back on my workload and, without making a big fuss about it, began working only part-time. This seems to create just the right balance. I am back to being at home when the girls come out of school, but at the same time I have a life of my own.

I realise now that I was too pushy – I was so desperately anxious to do the right thing, and as a result I put too much pressure on the girls. They both call me Mum now. I'm still cautious – I'm careful not to force my way into their lives, but wait to be asked. Essentially, though, we are now a Mum, Dad and two kids – we've made it!

Forging vital links

One of the saddest aspects of step-parenthood is that the positive side so rarely comes to light. For example, stepmothers often tend to be nearer their stepchildren's age than their natural parents since, depressingly, men usually change partners for a younger model. In this instance there is enormous scope for playing a vital role in your stepchildren's life – as a friend rather than as a parent. Clothes, music, drugs, sex, drink, cigarettes, relationships in general – all these subjects are so much more easily discussed with a near contemporary, particularly one who is not too emotionally involved to voice an unbiased opinion.

Pat was only twenty when she married Jamie, twenty-four years her senior:

I was really nervous the first time I met Jamie's son, Ed. It was such a crazy situation – Ed was two years older than me! He'd lived with his mother for most of his childhood and so Jamie and Ed weren't very close, but Jamie somehow felt he wanted his son's approval, which I could understand.

We met the first time in a wine bar. From the moment Ed walked in I could see he'd got problems. I've never used drugs, but I've got plenty of friends who have – and from one look at Ed, I could see he was into something heavy. It was a fairly difficult meeting – Ed was very on edge and fairly aggressive towards his father. He barely acknowledged I existed.

After he had gone, Jamie was very upset. He said he hadn't had a proper relationship with his son for years – they couldn't talk. Apparently Ed had been expelled from school and had never really had a job. Jamie seemed to blame his wife for everything, and was quite put out when I said that maybe he should have tried harder to get along with his son.

I suppose it was because we were arguing that I had the guts to tell him that Ed was on drugs. At first Jamie didn't believe me, but when I described the symptoms, which to me had been so obvious, I could see that in his heart of hearts Jamie had probably known, too. We talked about it all night.

In a funny kind of way it sort of brought us closer together, and the next day Jamie went off to Wiltshire to see his ex-wife. They had it out with Ed, and he is now in a rehabilitation clinic. He was on heroin but the prognosis is good – they reckon they might really be able to cure his addiction. He wants to be cured, that's the main thing. When he comes out, he's already said he'd like to come and live with us for a while.

We've been to see him quite a lot in the clinic. He seems to think it's rather a joke, his Dad and I being married. He calls me his little stepmum and I think he's quite tickled with the idea. I like him, he's a nice bloke. I think things might really work out for us as a family. I'm pregnant, too, and Ed's really excited about having a little brother or sister.

Pat's story is extreme in the sense that she is actually younger than her stepson. None the less, she could look beyond her husband's guilt at not being able to communicate with his son and see the cause of Ed's problems. The son was a drug addict, yet so beleaguered was his father with his own sense of failure that he had not spotted it, even though subconsciously he had known something was wrong.

A step-parent can often act as a diffuser of situations, a voice of reason while the natural parents are locked into court battles over money or custody. Step-parents can create around them a pool of tranquillity, a place where the children can find peace away from warring parents. For this reason it does help enormously if step-parents can try to ease the tension in squabbles between natural parents. Obviously the tendency is to give your partner full support, but if the interests of the children are to be considered first, steer clear if you can.

Extended families

In essence, don't concentrate on trying to be a good substitute parent to your stepchildren, but aim to be someone in your own right, a relationship set apart – not mother, not father, but an important, perhaps even vital, entity complete in itself. Emma, a very well-balanced only child of fourteen, said that the best thing that could possibly have happened to her was both her parents remarrying. As she put it:

> I now have two homes – one in London and one in the country. I still have Mummy and Daddy, but I also have Jane and William. This means I've got four people to look after me, and I have seven grandparents and a whole lot of new cousins. I'm also given far more Christmas and birthday presents than I used to have. Although I wish Mummy and Daddy had stayed together, I really like things the way they are now.

A great many stepchildren are not so gloriously uncomplicated, particularly at fourteen, but there is a lot of sound common sense in what Emma is saying. Given that her parents' marriage was doomed in any event, the only sensible way ahead is to look for the positive aspects, the plus points – in her case, the opportunity for town and country life and more people to care about her and make her feel secure, not to mention the touch of avarice . . . well, why not?

The extended family – the stepgrandparents,

stepaunts, uncles and cousins – can contribute enormously to the success or otherwise of a new stepfamily, as I recall from my own experience:

> I remember with huge gratitude being in the room when Alan, now my husband, telephoned his brother, Norman, to tell him that we were getting married. Alan mentioned that he was also going to become a stepfather to my five-year-old daughter, Lucy.
>
> Norman's response was swift. 'Wonderful!' he said, 'at last we're going to have a girl in the family.' At the time Norman had three sons and Alan two. This simple gesture of instantly giving Lucy a role and status within our new family was immeasurably reassuring. And it has certainly proved to be more than all talk. We have since had a son of our own by birth, and adopted another. The attitude of Norman and his wife, Joan, to all our children has been consistent and reassuring. They are a brilliant aunt and uncle to all of them, regardless of their origins.

Learning to cope

There are so many ways in which people become step-parents, and in so many different circumstances. It may be that your relationship has caused the break-up of your partner's marriage, in which case resentment from your stepchildren is almost inevitable. The children may come and live with you permanently, or be weekenders, or visit only in the school holidays. They may be very damaged by what they have experienced, they may harbour longings for their parents to be reunited, they may blame you for everything, or they may blame themselves. They may be babies or adolescents, or anything in between. You might find loving them easy or impossible; and even the concept of liking them may be a strain.

Even if you feel you have drawn a short straw, the decision to become involved is yours and you have to learn to cope. After all, natural parents suffer disappointments, too – sometimes terrible ones. Many a longed-for child has been born physically or mentally handicapped; many an adored baby has turned into a hopeless drug addict; many a much-loved son or daughter has been cut down, when their life has hardly begun, by disease or accident. Family life is never perfect – there are always stresses and strains. Even if you feel confident about what you are doing, do not expect too much. But once you have made your commitment you must learn to cope with it.

Bob's story demonstrates how a crisis can very quickly sort out priorities:

I met Jilly at a bad time in my life. I'd left my wife ten years before for another woman, but our relationship hadn't worked out. Since then there had been the odd casual girlfriend, but no one important. My two children were grown up and no longer needed me. My ex-wife had remarried and was happy. My mother had just died, and my business was going through a difficult patch. It suddenly seemed as though I had nothing and no one.

Then into my life came Jilly. She's fourteen years younger than me – pretty, vivacious and, for some inexplicable reason, apparently in love with me. She has a daughter, Emma, who was six when we met – pretty and bubbly like her mother. I could see no reason at all why I should not love this child as my own and we decided to get married, but within weeks of our marriage I was feeling bitterly resentful.

On so many occasions Jilly seemed to put Emma before me. She even insisted that the child came away on our honeymoon. I could understand her reasons – mother and daughter had never been parted before, and Jilly felt that Emma must not be left out at such an important moment.

Nevertheless the whole situation began to irritate me, and it was starting to affect my relationship with Emma. I simply didn't want the child around; that was the truth of it.

I came home late from work one night to find Jilly in a real state. Emma was running a very high temperature. She had suddenly become very poorly during the day – a sore throat, an aching neck and head.

I have to admit I thought Jilly was over-reacting as usual, fussing about the child instead of being interested in what had happened to me during the day. I poured myself a drink, and I remember moaning quite a lot about the fact that there was no supper. When I think about it now, my blood runs cold at how selfish I was.

By ten o'clock Emma was in considerable pain and virtually delirious, and even I was forced to admit that something was very wrong. We called the doctor, and she was admitted to hospital immediately with suspected meningitis.

I'll never forget sitting by her bedside with Jilly, willing her to live. It made me remember how I'd felt when my own children were small and they'd been hurt in just some small way – how I'd wished it had been me, not them. Suddenly it was if scales had been lifted from my eyes. I understood exactly what Jilly was feeling, what she was going through, and I realised how difficult the last weeks and months must have been for her. It must have felt to her like she had two children in the house, with me and Emma vying for each other's attention.

We lived through the next three days and nights not knowing whether Emma would live – and if she did, whether she would be brain-damaged. We didn't talk much – not then – but in our anguish we did draw closer together.

When the crisis was over, when we knew Emma would be all right and we were able to relax a little, it was like the opening of flood gates. Jilly told me how desperately miserable she had been about having to choose all the time between her daughter and me. She said how much she loved us both, but our needs were different and sometimes she just couldn't balance them both. I felt terrible, because I knew everything she said was right.

I realised with hindsight that I'd reacted rather as a starving man would do to unlimited food. I'd been on my own for so long that when I discovered Jilly loved me I wanted every moment of her time, every ounce of her love, for myself. I couldn't entertain the idea of having to share her. I explained this as best I could, knowing it was the most terrible admission of selfishness and jealousy, but miraculously she seemed to understand.

When Emma came out of hospital we started again, and since then things have been fine. As Jilly pointed out, if I wanted her I had to recognise that she and Emma were a package deal. I had to accept them both, be prepared to give my love to both of them, or recognise we had no future.

Talking things through is essential

One of the most important things a step-parent can help a family to achieve is good communication – really *talking*. When a marriage breaks down and children are involved, inevitably there is a lot of pain around. Everyone is treading on eggshells emotionally. It is likely that the parents can barely communicate without rowing, and the children are pawns in the middle, buffeted this way and that. Everyone becomes so sensitive and frankly so exhausted that they cannot cope with yet another scene, and so they take the easy way out. Talking banalities is very restful, even if the real issues are being ignored.

When Peter was twelve, he spent the first day of his half-term holiday from boarding school with his father and a pleasant enough young woman. She was by no means the first of his father's girlfriends whom Peter had met in the six years since his parents had split up.

It was while we were having supper that Dad suddenly announced that he and Sally were going to get married, and that in fact Sally would be staying for the whole weekend. He was very jolly about it all and opened a bottle of champagne.

At the time, all I could think was that I wished she wasn't staying for the weekend. Dad and I always did the same things at half-term, and she was going to get in the way.

Later, Dad came to my bedroom to say goodnight. He was still very jolly and said how pleased he was that I liked Sally, and how glad he was that I was happy about them getting married.

I didn't say anything, but I was very angry. I hadn't said I was pleased they were getting married. I wasn't pleased. I had always hoped that Mum and Dad would get married again one day, and Sally was going to ruin all that. He hadn't even asked me what I thought – he had just decided I was pleased, when I wasn't at all. That night I really hated Sally.

It is a situation which we can all understand. The father, desperate for his son to like his fiancée, creates his own acceptable version of how his son thinks. So pleased was Peter's father with his own new-found happiness that he gave little or no thought as to how to break the news to Peter.

This is perhaps the time when a sensitive future step-mother could have pointed out the need to take things slowly, and to explain that, when the news was broken, father and son should have been alone so that Peter had the opportunity to express his doubts freely. Instead, the whole relationship started on the wrong footing because Peter's goodwill was assumed. Father and son just failed to communicate.

Avoiding disorientation

It is difficult, of course, to exert yourself in a new relationship when it comes to handling children, particularly if you have not had children of your own. You meet a man or woman whom you want to marry, and there is enough going on with the excitement and discovery of a new relationship without having to learn to be a parent as well.

A trivial incident shows how totally unprepared I was to be a parent:

When I first got married I was very young and yet instantly inherited two teenage stepsons. I remember to this day going out with my future husband and sons for the first time. Alastair opened the rear door of the car and I began climbing in. 'What are you doing?' he asked. 'You're supposed to sit in the front – the children sit in the back.' Because he was older than me – indeed he had been a friend of my parents – I instantly cast myself in the role of the child. I was terribly embarrassed, and the boys sniggered a great deal.

11

This disorientation factor is very common amongst new step-parents – one moment you are single, and the next you find yourself not only with a partner, but with a ready-made family.

For this reason it is vital to look at your potential new status with the blinkers off. You cannot separate your new relationship from your future partner's children. To ignore or underestimate the parental status – that way, madness lies. Loving other people's children is not so hard if you are properly prepared for it.

2

Marriage Break-ups

It may seem inappropriate, in a book devoted to step-parents, to include a chapter on the break-up of marriages. But when infidelity is the main cause, in over sixty per cent of broken marriages the unfaithful partner does not go on to marry the person who caused the split in the first place. In other words, in such situations it often takes one relationship to destroy the marriage and another to create a second marriage. As a result, many step-parents have no knowledge of what actually happened during their partner's divorce proceedings and therefore cannot fully appreciate the pain and long-term damage which may have been caused to the children, and indeed to both marriage partners.

The object of this chapter is to explain briefly the procedure for divorce when children are involved, so that step-parents can readily understand the strain – both emotional and financial – that is placed on a divorcing couple. This story from June highlights the trauma of this time for children.

The fact that I, too, came from a broken home undoubtedly helped my relationship with my stepchildren. My parents divorced at a time when family break-ups were fairly rare – certainly no one else in my class at school had divorced parents. It was all very messy and bitter, and I seemed to be unhappy for years.

When I met Tim's children for the first time, it was like looking into a mirror of my own childhood. I could see in their faces what they'd been through. And here was I, one more new thing to cope with – a potential stepmother.

Straightaway I told them of my own past. I was able to explain how I'd felt, and they kept saying, 'That's how we feel, too.' I was also able to explain things to Tim which he hadn't understood or appreciated, because he'd never experienced it from a child's point of view.

It's not that I'm a particularly clever or sensitive person, but I suppose few people realise just how heartbreaking your parents' divorce can be – unless, of course, it's happened to you.

The new Children Act

Without doubt, one of the greatest factors to have had an impact on the children of divorcing parents is the 1989 Children Act, which came into effect on 14 October 1991 and applies to the whole United Kingdom. Its aim is to try and reduce conflict between parents and to avoid the distressing and often expensive legal battles which were so common in the past where custody of children was being decided. To this end, all judges and magistrates who hear cases relating to children are now having to undergo extensive training on the law and the special considerations which arise from children's cases. Conciliation is now the name of the game.

Under the old law, when a court was dealing with separation or divorce proceedings it was obliged to consider the needs of the children. In nearly all instances it directed that one parent should have care and control of the children while the other had access. The court also usually directed that parents should have joint custody of their children, although in some cases custody was awarded to one parent only. Custody gave parents the right to a say on all major issues such as schooling, religion, general upbringing and medical treatment.

Under the new Act, the court is only required to make an order dealing with children if it considers that one is necessary. It will no longer award custody to one or other parent. Instead, both parents will retain parental responsibility for their children and therefore will maintain the right to have their views considered in any major decision affecting their offspring. The new legislation also means that both parents will remain responsible for ensuring the proper upbringing of their children. In many cases, if there is no major conflict between parents – when they have already agreed between themselves where their children should live and how often the other parent should visit – the court will be quite happy to abide by the parents' arrangements and make no order at all.

The arrangements are set out in advance of the court hearing in a very comprehensive form to be completed by both partners, and this document forms the basis of their agreement. This, of course, is the ideal situation. It allows flexibility and minimum interference by the court in what, ideally, should be something that children and parents work out for themselves.

However, if there is a parental dispute about the children the court will make a Residence Order, directing with which parent the children should live. It replaces the older Care and Control Order. Under the new law, the parent with the Residence Order will no longer need to apply for permission to take the child abroad, provided it is for a period of no more than a month at a time. However, the parent without the Residence Order will need to apply for permission. In addition the court will make a Contact Order, indicating how and when the other parent may visit the children or indeed communicate with them via letters or telephone calls – this replaces the old Access Order.

The court also has the right to make a Prohibited Steps Order, preventing parents or other people concerned with the children's lives from taking particular action without the court's permission. Specific issues orders can also be made to regularise particular areas of dispute relating to the child.

No rights for step-parents
Unmarried fathers do not have automatic rights, although they may apply to the court to be granted Parental Responsibility and any other type of order already referred to. This also applies to anyone with a

legitimate interest in the child's welfare – grandparents, foster parents and indeed step-parents all have the right to apply for either a Residence or Contact Order if they have been involved over a lengthy period in the care of a child.

It has to be said, though, that in the case of grandparents age will count against them: it is unlikely that the court would grant them a Residence Order unless they are particularly young for their role (i.e. in their forties). It is also an important point that step-parents have no legal status whatsoever with regard to their stepchildren. In the event of a death or divorce, it is necessary for a step-parent to prove the importance of his or her role in the stepchild's life in order to gain access to him or her. A step-parent has no automatic rights at all, however long he or she may have cared for the child. Angela voices the fears of many parents who recognise this situation:

When Ben and I got married, his becoming stepfather to my children was not a problem. The boys were two and three at the time, and I knew right from the beginning that, as far as Ben was concerned, they were his kids, too, and he loved them. I know other people have all sorts of difficulties, and I realise that I am really lucky with Ben – and so are my two boys.

In a funny way, it was because Ben was such a good stepfather that I worried about the boys so much. Henry, my first husband, is an absolute slob – he lies, cheats and is a terrible drunkard. He was always letting the children down – he never remembered their birthdays, that sort of thing.

What used to haunt me, all during the boys' childhood, was what would happen if I died. If the boys were allowed to stay with Ben, then I knew they would be well cared for and above all loved. Although obviously it would be a big disruption in their lives, essentially their childhood would remain intact. If, however, they'd been forced to go and live with Henry I just dread to think what would happen to them.

We looked at various ways of trying to protect the boys in case of such an eventuality. But there were no guarantees, no ways of ensuring that Ben would be allowed to keep them if I died, unless he adopted them. And Henry would never have agreed to that. They're grown up now, but the worry used to keep me awake at night.

Appointing guardians can alleviate much of this worry – your solicitor will help you with the detail. In addition, Chapter 7 contains more about adoption by step-parents.

'Too many bedrooms'

Where there is a particularly bitter dispute as to how much contact a parent should have with his or her children, the court has the power to make a Split Residence Order. It might state, for example, that the children should live with one parent during the term and another during the holidays, or one during the week and the other at weekends. This seems to be bending over backwards to be fair to the parents. Children should surely have one main home, centred on their school and friends, to give them stability and a sense of belonging. Of course this is not 'fair' to the other parent – but then divorce is not very fair on anyone, particularly the children. I think there is nothing more damaging than dreadful wrangles between parents which end in the poor child being pushed from pillar to post. Here is a sad example:

> A friend of ours has a little girl who was having serious emotional problems at eleven, following her parents' divorce. The child psychiatrist who examined her said she was suffering from 'too many bedrooms in her life'. At the time, Anna was at boarding school – a typical half-term of four days, when she desperately needed to relax after the rigours of communal life, would be spent two nights with Daddy and two nights with Mummy, with a hundred-mile journey between the two.

Such a decision might be fine for the parents but desparately unfair on the child, who seems to be doled out in equal amounts to keep everyone happy. As a step-parent you might well be able to spot such a situation and perhaps help your partner work out a formula which is less demanding on the child.

Even without wrangling, children can be put in impossible situations. This grandmother's story is interesting:

I know I should be pleased by the way in which my son Richard and his wife, Mary, split up. They are so open-handed and co-operative to one another in their attitude to Diana, their only child, who was seven at the time of their divorce.

It is all very organised – during termtime Diana lives with her mother and spends every weekend with her father. In the holidays she lives with her father and spends every weekend with her mother – that is except for the first and last weekend in the month, when she goes to her maternal grandmother's on the first weekend and me on the last. Everyone is happy with this arrangement – it is fair and equitable in every way.

Fair to everyone, in my mind, except Diana. She is being carved up, so that everyone has a fair piece of her. No one argues, because everyone is satisfied with their lot; but nobody asks Diana how she feels. Sometimes when she comes to me she seems so tired. The trouble is she has no real home – she's just sent round like a package. I know it's not a good idea, parents scrapping over their children, but at least it demonstrates that they care.

I feel Richard and Mary have behaved in an almost unnatural way, falling over backwards to allow each other to have time with their child, almost as if neither of them really want her.

I wonder what will happen when she's older and she wants to spend time with her friends at weekends when she's supposed to be on the move? She's going to have to be a brave girl to tackle that one. She appears happy enough on the surface, I can't deny that, but I really believe that in everyone's efforts to be fair, no one has really considered Diana's view.

The cost of it all
Now to the thorny question of money, and one thing is

absolutely certain: if you want to get rich, you should not get divorced.

I had no idea it was going to be so hard, financially. I was fed up with my husband's infidelity – there had been one woman after another all through our married life. It was so insulting. Finally, when the children were eight and eleven and I felt they were old enough to know what was going on, I told him to get out.

That's when our problems really started – the maintenance order was inadequate and in any case my husband rarely paid it, and my job simply could not support the children and the house. So we sold the house and bought something smaller. And then my husband started squabbling about his share of the so-called profit we'd made.

The children hated the new house – it was miles from their friends – and, to be honest, so did I. We no longer had a garden and so we had to find a home for the dog, and the cat was run over just a few weeks after we moved in. It was like our whole world was destroyed. I don't mind admitting I often regret my decision, and I'm sure the children blame me for ruining their lives.

Having two homes where once there was one, having two lots of toys, beds and general equipment for the children, not to mention the cost of journeys between both homes, telephone calls and so on, places an enormous financial burden on the former family. It does not matter who was responsible for the break-up of the marriage, who is in the right, who has the children, who is earning the major share of the income – everybody loses. The problem in the average family is that there is never enough money to go round.

It is all very well for the aggrieved wife, trying to raise two children alone, to moan that the maintenance she receives from her former husband is not enough. He has to live, he has to have a roof over his head, clothes on his back and the ability to get to work.

Equally, it is unreasonable for the husband to expect his former wife to abandon traumatised children to a full-time child minder while she goes out to work to try and make up the shortfall.

Increasingly, where no children are involved, courts tend to end marriages with a financial agreement which gives a clean break. In other words, rather than a husband continuing to pay maintenance into the sunset to a woman without children, she is awarded a fair share of the existing capital and as a result their financial relationship is at an end. This is by far the most satisfactory arrangement, because it means that the wife is assured of receiving what is hers by right and dispenses with the prospect of future wrangling if maintenance payments are stopped because of dispute or a change of circumstances.

However, this situation is not a luxury that parents with children can normally enjoy. As already mentioned, at the time of deciding to get divorced each parent is asked to fill out a form which not only details the arrangements they wish to make for the children but also provides comprehensive information on their financial circumstances. Once again the primary concern of the court is the needs of the children.

In the past it was commonly believed that, in disputes over money, step-parents could be involved in supporting their partner's previous family. This is not the case, and indeed it never has been. In certain circumstances where there is a financial dispute after one or both partners has remarried, the step-parents may be asked by the court to disclose their income. There is no suggestion that the step-parent should be expected to support the partner's family, simply that their income will be taken into account when trying to balance the books in both households. None the less, occasionally step-parents do find themselves involved, as in Eleanor's case:

When Ian lost his job I saw it as part of my duty to ensure that

20

the maintenance cheques to his ex-wife continued to be paid. Her children were still very young at the time and there was no way she could sensibly have a full-time job. I have a very well-paid job, and although things were tight I did still manage to cover the mortgage as well. Ian managed our living expenses from his redundancy money.

When one or two of our friends heard what I was doing they thought I was mad, because of course it wasn't my responsibility. I just didn't see it like that. Ian and I were married, for better or for worse. He had hit hard times, and one of his commitments was his support to his ex-wife. It was just the same as paying the electricity or telephone bill – it was something that had to be done. When Ian got a new job he said he wanted to pay me back but I resisted it, because it really wasn't important. I'd like to think he'd have done the same for me.

Ian is a lucky man – not every wife would have taken this view. For whatever reason, Eleanor clearly does not resent Ian's former wife or consider her requirements for financial support unreasonable. If more people could find themselves able to take this attitude, the children would benefit hugely – and not just in financial terms.

Destroyer of relationships

Money is not simply a problem because it is in short supply. It is also a problem because it acts as a constant reminder of what went before, binding any new relationships to the old one, underlining the fact that once there was a family which has now broken apart. Money or, more often than not, the lack of it draws attention to the fact that one or both parents are irrevocably linked to their former family, and it has a nasty way of upsetting the balance of often very fragile relationships – even destroying them altogether. Take Coral's experience:

John, my second husband, is a very honest, straightforward, reliable man. It's one of the things I love about him most, because he is such a contrast to Mark, my first husband, who has very little sense of responsibility.

John has two boys, Peter and Edward, by his previous marriage. They live with their mother, although they visit us frequently. John is absolutely reliable in the maintenance payments he gives Betty for the boys – he has never let her down once, and if she makes special requests for extra money for school trips or whatever, he always finds it even if we have to go without.

I don't resent this, not at all – I respect his sense of obligation towards his sons. The problem is that Mark has never paid a penny of maintenance towards Tom, our son, who lives permanently with me. He promises to do so, and I have taken him to court on several occasions, but nothing substantial or regular has ever occurred. It makes me feel so feckless, so irresponsible, although I recognise I am probably being hypersensitive. It's just that poor old John has to support Tom as well as his own two boys, and although I work full-time I somehow feel it's not enough. John can't shirk his responsibilities it's so unfair, and somehow I feel it's all my fault.

Coral then goes on to highlight the problems experienced in many families where a huband may feel overburdened by the requirements to support everyone. The strain of so doing may cause resentment and bitterness, which in turn may affect relationships with the children, however unreasonable this may be.

I'm sure John's relationship with Tom is affected by the lack of maintenance. He really seems to resent my son and avoids him as much as he can.

Human nature being what it is, rare is the wife who feels she is receiving enough maintenance to support her children, and rare the husband who does not feel hard done by because of the amount he is expected to pay. One of the major grouses of second wives is that they are often denied the chance of having children of their own. This is because the amount of maintenance their husbands have to pay for their first families renders it necessary for both partners to work full-time to make ends meet.

Obviously this is a very genuine concern, but it goes without saying that the responsibility for existing children must be paramount. A second wife has to understand that her husband has to support his existing children. If she does not like it, she should not go ahead with the marriage.

Sometimes financial considerations confuse the issue, as in Laura's case:

> When the subject of marriage came up I asked him about children, naturally assuming that he would like some. Since he had two already, I had always assumed he liked kids.
>
> His reply really shocked me – he was absolutely adamant that he didn't want any more children. I couldn't understand it. His were virtually grown up, and he had seen little of their childhood because he and his wife had been not only divorced but estranged for many years. I thought he'd love the opportunity to start again.
>
> He said he didn't want another family because he simply couldn't bear to cope with the financial commitment again, particularly at his age. Somehow it didn't ring true – he was normally so generous by nature. His attitude alarmed me. If I really knew him so little, should I be marrying him at all?
>
> One night I broke down and told him how much I wanted children – not just children but his children, and I wasn't sure I could marry him if he was against having them. It was a very stormy evening, and it was some hours before he finally opened up and admitted what the real problem was.
>
> He had found the pain of essentially losing his children, when they were so young, too much to bear. His wife had remarried, and the children regarded their stepfather as their true father. He had just not thought it right to be a disruptive influence in the new family group, and had therefore played a very minor role in their growing up and was terrified of the same thing happening again. In other words, he was frightened to take the emotional risk. Money simply didn't come into it.

I reassured him in every way I could. We now have two lovely children and a very happy marriage.

Sensibly, Laura did not let herself become involved in the idea of marriage until she really understood how her future husband felt. The true reason for their differences was not money-related, even though it purported to be.

Whatever the cause, such differences must be ironed out at an early stage. This is why it is so important to understand the financial implications of your partner's responsibilities before your relationship develops too far. It may sound unromantic, but it is a necessity. When two young people fall in love, without any commitments on either side, the only thing they have to consider is each other and whether they want to spend the rest of their lives together. When a couple with children and former relationships to consider fall in love, practial considerations have to play a major part. Love's young dream is, sadly, not enough.

When the children bear the brunt

Older children and adolescents can become very frustrated by arguments over money, particularly if they have spent years listening to their parents haggle and moan. Children often have a greater understanding of the likely financial burden they impose than they are normally given credit for, and would like to know how much money is available, how much it costs to support them and so on. If they ask, involve them in the financial juggling act – but without being melodramatic and without making them feel insecure. An understanding of how difficult it is to balance the books will do them no harm at all, although it may open the doors to a degree of criticism. Jenny was eight when her parents divorced, and fifteen when she spoke to me:

> I live with my Mum, in the house she used to share with Dad – in fact I've lived here all my life. Apart from the house, the one other constant factor throughout my childhood has been my

mother moaning about how mean my father is and how little money he gives her to maintain me.

It just doesn't stack up from where I'm standing – Mum has a well-paid job, we live in a nice house, we have holidays, clothes and a car, and she's often out with friends. Dad lives in this miserable flat, with his girlfriend Alice and their baby. Alice can't work because the baby is only small, and I can just tell they're really poor. I think they're poor because Dad has to give all his money to Mum, and I feel guilty about that because it's for me really. Once I leave school I'll earn my own money, and then Dad can keep his.

Meantime, though, I worry about my half-brother, Eddie, and whether Dad's going to manage to support us all. I think my Mum lives in cloud cuckoo land. I asked her once to let me know how much maintenance she received. She went completely mad and didn't speak to me for several days. But then she's never seen how Dad lives, she's never been there, so she can't imagine what she's doing to him.

This sort of situation puts an intolerable strain on the child. The parents here are so locked into their own problems that they fail to see how Jenny is bearing the brunt of their financial wrangles. She is starting to feel guilty about her very existence – an existence which makes it necessary for her father and his new family to live in relative poverty. She worries about her new little brother. Maybe she is a particularly caring and sensitive child, but why are her parents so blind to the suffering they are causing her?

It would be helpful if her mother could see how her father is living – though, of course, this is unlikely to happen. It would be helpful, too, if her mother could discuss some of the financial details of their lives, particularly since over the years she seems to have involved Jenny, albeit negatively, with her apparently incessant moaning. This situation, if allowed to continue, may seriously undermine Jenny's sense of self-worth in the long term. Yet her parents seem completely unaware of her feelings.

This leads to the overall question of dispute between parents, whether it is financial or where the children should live. Childhood is so brief, and it is so easy for constantly arguing parents to destroy it for their children. If a real battle has to take place, because parents cannot agree on the arrangements for their children, a court welfare officer is usually appointed. The officer interviews the children and both parents, and submits a report to the court. A date for a hearing will be set, where a judge in chambers will attempt to unravel the dispute and settle it once and for all. His major concern will be the best interests of the children – first, their upbringing, and second, their financial support.

However, all this takes time. While it is going on everyone is in a state of limbo and the atmosphere is likely to be tense and full of aggravation, which is very hard on the child. Joanna was eleven at the time of her parents' divorce and is now in her mid-thirties:

I couldn't bear it! After the split I still got on very well with my parents individually, but together they were awful. All the aggravation was just terrible – they couldn't seem to say a single civil word to each other, and of course they used me all the time in their battles.

I used to go to enormous lengths to avoid them meeting. I tried to draw up a timetable so that they each came to different events at school, and I would contrive to be spending the day with a friend when I was handed from one parent to the other, so at least I had moral support.

Looking back on it, there was relatively little pain associated with my parents splitting up. I didn't mind having two homes and all the other disruptions that went with it – children on the whole accept these things. What I couldn't stand was the disputes and arguing and court cases, particularly since most of them revolved round me. I just wanted them to stop and to leave me and each other alone. I wanted to have conversations with each of them that didn't end up like the Spanish Inquisition, each quizzing me as to what the other one was up to.

Sometimes when I looked at other people's parents hugging each other, being kind to one another, I wanted to kill my Mum and Dad. It's all so long ago now, but I can never forgive them for what they did – never.

Of course there are some marriages where one partner's behaviour is so unacceptable that the other is forced to take a stand to protect the children. However, in most instances neither partner is the villain, yet each side allows bitterness and aggravation to escalate to the point where it causes untold damage to their children – and indeed to themselves.

As a future step-parent, if you have any influence at all, diffusing this sort of situation could prove of invaluable help to the children. Of course you will have to be careful, because your partner may well view your efforts at conciliation as disloyalty. None the less you are in a unique position. You are not directly involved in the dispute, but you are going to have to live with its results for the rest of your life. Being one step removed, you may well be able to see the damage being caused to the children which their own parents cannot see; and, what is more, you may be able to do something to help the situation.

Children's power

Children rarely appreciate just how much power they have – they tend to suffer in silence, feeling that the whole dispute is an adult affair that they cannot influence themselves.

But one of the interesting effects of the Children Act is that, since more emphasis is being placed on the needs and wants of the child, children could quite literally take the law into their own hands. A child has a right to Legal Aid, and can instruct a solicitor. In the years ahead older children may well apply to the court for the right to live with one parent or the other, or indeed ask the court to stop the unwanted interference of a parent. The fact that children have this power may encourage parents to listen to what their children want. If they do not, at least children now have some redress.

Barry's mother felt that her son was suffering greatly from his access visits to his father, Ted, and decided to do something about it. For a long time the boy had been unhappy about going to see his father. His behaviour began to deteriorate several days before he was due to go on a visit, and when he came back he was always tired and subdued for at least a week. He was having hardly any normal life at all – he was either getting over the last visit or dreading the next one.

> One day I asked him outright whether he wanted to go on seeing his father. It was like opening the flood gates. He was twelve by then but he cried like a baby, on and on. He said how much he hated his father, that his father was always getting at him – being horrible about me and his stepdad and on several occasions Ted has actually hit him when he wouldn't agree with something abusive he'd said about me. It's not as though Barry was a little kid – he was old enough to know his own mind.
>
> We went and talked to a solicitor, and in turn a welfare officer was appointed. He talked the whole thing through with Barry and his dad and, of course, with me. He said it would be nice if some sort of contact was maintained, either by letter or phone, but said the boy should not have to go and see Ted unless he wanted to. Like me, he agreed he was old enough to know his own mind and said he was confident that I was not influencing the boy's decision.

Comparatively few children would feel able to tackle any form of court hearing unless forced to do so. However, just knowing that they have the ability to take action can be no bad thing. Over and over again, one sees parents in such a state of conflict and bitterness that their children's wishes are simply of no relevance. The fight is all.

I have not attempted to go into detail about the carve-up of a marriage – there are so many other considerations to take into account, such as pensions, insurance policies and the ghastly dividing of personal effects. But this is not a chapter on how to get a divorce.

Put yourself in the position of the children involved in a marriage break-up. Even if the atmosphere in the family home has not been good for some time, certain rituals will have gone on for as long as the children can remember. They make almost any amount of friction better than the breakdown of the family. Dad takes them to the park on Saturday morning while Mum does the shopping. They all go to see Granny on Sunday afternoons. Dad gives them their bath and Mum reads them their bedtime story. . . .

Suddenly this is all at an end. Everything is turned upside down, with their mother or father leaving the family home. While still reeling from shock the children are expected to cope with the sale of their home and a move to a new house or flat which will almost certainly be inferior. Perhaps they will have to go to a new school. Perhaps they will be living too far away to visit their friends on a regular basis. 'No, the climbing frame will have to go since we haven't got a garden now. . . . No, we're not going to Spain again this year – we can't afford it. . . . No, you won't be going to ballet classes next term – they don't run them at your new school.'

There may be plus points, but they are very hard to imagine. Children do not like change – even babies react badly to it. They like a structured routine, and if they are given bucketfuls of security and stability as a base they will flourish and learn to make their own way in the world with confidence. If the very fabric of their life is destroyed they trust nothing, for there is nothing left to fall back on.

You may well find yourself in a position where you are taking on children who have been through this sort of trauma. What they desperately need is something sure and certain in their lives – and that person could quite possibly be you.

3

Getting It Together

Social workers employ a device to help prospective foster and adoptive parents understand some of the problems which may be upsetting their children. They ask them to think back to a painful incident in their own life which caused a loss of security, and try to remember how it felt. Even if you led a relatively trauma-free childhood – if your parents stayed married, you enjoyed a happy relationship with your siblings and you never wanted for anything – there will still be incidents which caused you intense grief.

In my case the best example was going to boarding school. My parents sent me at eleven, and although I was on the whole happy there, the initial feeling of disorientation and dislocation was intense. It was not helped by the fact that I was an only child and very shy. Everything that I had taken for granted in my safe, secure world up to that point was at an end; everything was now new and uncertain.

As a prospective step-parent, go through this exercise and ask your partner to do the same thing. Try and remember precisely how it felt to be small and vulnerable and, above all, not in charge. There are huge disadvantages in being an adult, but one of the few advantages is that we are more or less masters of our own destiny. If we decide to ruin our lives, that's up to us. Jeffery has first-hand experience of how easy it is to destroy a child's life. Happily remarried now, he will never be able to escape his guilt about the past.

I will never forget the moment when I suddenly realised the appalling impact our marriage break-up was having on our son. Although my wife and I were very bitter about our parting, we both loved Timothy very much indeed. We had taken great care to explain to him that, although he would be living mostly with his mother in future, I would visit him regularly and that we both still loved him as much as ever. We explained it all together, and separately, and he seemed to understand – although of course it is difficult to tell how much a child of only six understands.

The first time I came to take him out, he began to cry almost as soon as we drove off. For a while he wouldn't tell me what was wrong. Then eventually he said, 'When Mummy stops loving me I suppose I can come and live with you. But what will happen to me when you stop loving me?'

To start with, I couldn't understand what he was getting at. I thought that maybe his mother had been bitching about me and sowing seeds of doubt about me in his mind.

I was so angry I was ready to tear her to pieces, but I controlled myself and asked him to try and explain.

The truth was far more ghastly than any bitching on my wife's part. Timothy had decided that love was only a transient thing – that it was not for ever. After all, his mother and father loved one another, and then that love had died. He therefore now assumed that sooner or later his mother would stop loving him and that she would want him to go, just like I had. He'd worked out that he could come to me, but when I stopped loving him – what next?

The appalling vulnerability of his situation had me in tears as well. I stopped the car and tried to explain that nothing would ever stop us loving him. But why should he believe me? He had logic on his side – love dies. He was only six, but he knew that. Why should he trust in an emotion which had destroyed everything that up to that moment he'd taken for granted?

Timothy's feelings couldn't bring his mother and me together again – our relationship had deteriorated too far. But when, later that night, I explained to her what he'd told me, she was as appalled as I was. From that day on, we were totally at one in committing ourselves to making sure that Timothy always felt secure.

We have both remarried now. Timothy is twelve and seems

31

to have adjusted well. But there is always in him, I believe, an inner sadness – he will never again be the merry little boy he was, before his mother and I wrecked his childhood. We have to live with that, and it's not easy.

Pitfalls for prospective step-parents

Children are vulnerable because they are so powerless. They are only too aware of this, and it heightens their sense of fear. They may have just been through their parents' separation and divorce and are feeling insecure anyway; then on to the scene comes a new prospective partner, for one or perhaps both their parents. There are various emotions they are likely to feel:

* Firstly, almost any new relationship into which one of their parents enters represents a threat to the children. If you, the prospective new step-parent, live, say, twenty miles from the home of the child and his parent, the child will begin to wonder whether, if your relationship becomes permanent, he will be expected to go and live in your house. Will he have to change his school? Will he lose his friends? If the child is old enough, he may consider the possibility of his parent's new relationship ending in the birth of another child and wonders how this will affect him.

   'Maybe, if Mummy has a new baby, she won't want me around any more and I'll have to go and live with Daddy. Maybe, as Daddy has a new girlfriend, he won't want me any more either.'

   In other words, recognise right from the beginning that your very existence is likely to cause pain. It is not a happy thought, but the better for being acknowledged. Your job, and the job of your partner, is to reassure the child that, from his or her point of view, things will either stay the same or definitely get better.

* The child may find your relationship with his or her parent deeply embarrassing, even revolting. As they get older, children find the concept of their parents

being involved in any kind of sexual activity at best ludicrous, and at worst downright disgusting. This particularly applies to mothers – mothers are supposed to be apple-cheeked paragons devoted to making delicious meals for their families! It may not be accurate, but it reflects the ideal. Certainly, entering into a blatantly sexual relationship with the parent of any child over seven is asking for resentment and ridicule. When you are with your partner and his or her children, imagine you are in the presence of an aged maiden aunt and act accordingly!

* Forget the big issues about who is going to live where and with whom – the fabric of a child's life is made up of small rituals. Crumpets for tea on Saturday afternoon, Granny's for lunch on Sunday, fishing trips, visits to the zoo, special food for special days may seem trivial but they are vital for security and continuity. A well-meaning step-parent can cause untold problems by making such offers as: 'So, you always have baked beans for tea when you come and visit Daddy – that's a bit boring, isn't it? Let's see if we can come up with something more exotic.' The child wants baked beans for tea with Daddy because that's what he always has. It is so easy to tread on toes and cause damage way out of proportion to the size of the incident – and all in a desperate effort to please.

* It is very easy for a prospective step-parent to be too competitive with the equivalent natural parent, sometimes completely subconsciously. If you, as the step-mother, are prettier and slimmer than the child's natural mother, you could find yourself taking enormous care with your appearance as if to emphasise the difference. If you are a better cook, have more money to spend on nice presents, live in a bigger house or drive a smarter car than the natural mother, you may consciously or unconsciously flaunt this aspect of your life to your prospective stepchild in an

effort to win him over. In the short term, it may seem to work. Children are easily seduced, particularly by material things, but you may find this approach rebounds on you. Don't say things like: 'Mummy would look really nice in 501s like yours, but she has to buy her jeans at the market because she can't afford any decent ones.'

The child's desire to protect his natural parent will be considerable, particularly if that parent is still single and apparently not having too good a time. Many people do not appreciate that even quite young children feel a tremendous sense of responsibility towards their single parent. Your efforts to shine may well be construed as criticism and cause deep resentment. This does not mean that you have to stick to fish fingers even if your boeuf en croûte is truly memorable – just don't flaunt it!

* As an extension of this point, don't be critical of your prospective stepchildren's parents. Clearly you should not criticise the parent of the same sex as yourself, but be equally careful about criticising your future partner, even if the child is aware of how much you love that person. In an effort to become closer to the child you might find yourself saying: 'Don't worry. I know Dad said you can't have the money for a skiing holiday, but he can be a bit of an old meanie – leave it to me, I'll twist his arm.'

On the face of it, siding with the child to get something that he or she wants should be a recipe for success. It rarely is, for it displays a worrying lack of loyalty. You may not be a parent, but you are part of the parent generation. As such you are supposed to close ranks and present a united front. Only in this way can rules be laid down and obeyed; and, more important, only in this way can children be helped to feel secure. If one adult is saying one thing and the other taking the opposite view, even over small issues, children get confused. And they will, of course, feel protective towards their natural parent. 'Who is this woman,' the child may well think, 'who dares criticise my father and tell me, his daughter, that he's mean with money? I've known him a lot longer than she has.' It's a perfectly natural and justifiable reaction.

* By the same token, don't work too hard at being fair. If the moment a prospective stepchild walks through your front door you suggest he rings his mother, your efforts to do the decent thing will be construed as interference and unwanted pressure. Of course – particularly if it is your house – you can tell the child that he should feel free to use the phone (or not, of course, if you are on a very tight budget), but don't lean over backwards to praise the other parent or emphasise too strongly your desire to be on friendly terms. The child will smell a rat and consider your reaction suspect and false. He will probably be right.

* It is essential to respect children's need for exclusive time with their natural parent. Don't crowd them, – leave them alone sometimes. Many step-parents seem to treat their partners as their own private property and enormously resent the time their partner spends with his or her children. Right from the beginning of your relationship, understand that if you are marrying someone with children you will never have them 100 per cent – if you do, there is something wrong with them. You have to cultivate a lot of tact to deal with this satisfactorily.

Let us take a hypothetical situation – supposing you are involved with a man who has a young son who is cricket-mad. The boy plays cricket for his school most Saturday afternoons, and traditionally father has gone along to watch the match. You do not stress your fascination with the game and ask to go too. Ideally you should find yourself something equally spellbinding to do on Saturday afternoons.

If, however, you genuinely enjoy cricket, suggest

you make the sandwiches for their picnic. After a few weeks of much-improved picnics and a gentle interest in their achievements, they might decide to ask you along. Go once, but then make it absolutely clear that you do not expect to be asked on a regular basis and arrange to do something yourself the following week. If they repeat the invitation, it probably means that they genuinely do want you to come again. So by all means go, but not every week – give them time alone.

It's not just the match itself – the drive to and from school and all the associated paraphernalia concerning equipment and after-match talk offer a wonderful chance for father and son to communicate. Leave them to it.

No winners
Any new relationship is vulnerable. A relationship where one or both partners has been recently and severely hurt by the breakdown of a marriage is particularly tricky – the wounded party is only too aware of how easily things can go wrong and how severe the consequences can be. Add to this the complication of possibly hostile children, and the result is a minefield.

Now a mother herself, Sarah feels remorse at her behaviour as a child:

> Looking back on it now, of course, I realise my sister Jane and I were absolute monsters. Daddy walked out when we were quite young – four or five – and for several years we lived with Mummy on our own, very happily, or so we thought. Of course now I can see that she was young, only in her late twenties, and it was ludicrous to expect her to spend the rest of her life bringing up her children alone. But of course when you're a child you can only see things from your own point of view.
>
> We didn't like Bernard from the beginning. He was falsely jolly with us and we could tell, as children can, that he didn't really like us. We were appalled when Mummy said she was going to marry him and, worse still, move to his house. Quite cold-bloodedly Jane and I set out to wreck their relationship.

We ignored Bernard as much as possible and stirred up rows between him and Mummy, and in the end I suppose we won – they parted after only about two years of marriage.

She never rebuked us, and right up to the day she died she gave us no indication that the breakdown of her marriage was our fault. Sometimes I like to try and convince myself that we knew best and saved her from years of misery. But looking back on it, a lot of what Bernard did was very kind and thoughtful – he probably wasn't such a bad bloke. It distresses me to think that Mother never had another serious man in her life, and I'm sure Jane and I are responsible for that. Her experiences with Bernard, following the breakdown of her marriage to our father, just destroyed her confidence. Her life was a failure really, and a lot of it was our fault.

Very early in the relationship, decide how far you are prepared to go despite the children. In other words, do you love and want this person enough that, however awful the children may appear to be, you will want to pursue the relationship? Most parents say they would not relentlessly pursue a relationship which had the strong disapproval of their children. By contrast, most step-parents say that hostile children would not have stopped them from pursuing the relationship – they might have been a threat, but not an irrevocable one. This interesting difference of viewpoint is open to all sorts of interpretations. I can't help feeling that the parent's view is the more realistic.

No one should necessarily expect step-parents to love their stepchildren automatically and instantly, but it is necessary to be kind. If you feel you cannot be kind to any prospective stepchildren, you should end the relationship and find an unattached partner. In other words, don't get in too deep for anyone's sake, unless you feel relatively confident that you are going to be able to handle your partner's children.

Betty was thirty-four when she met Henry, a man ten years older than her. He had three teenage daughters.

His wife had died of cancer when the youngest girl was only six and he had struggled on alone, with the help of a housekeeper, for seven years:

Henry and I met at the tennis club. I had belonged for some time and he joined because his doctor said he needed to get fit. I was unmarried, and at first I was wary of Henry's position as a widower with three children. However, the attraction between us was instant and I tended not to think too much about his family during our early meetings.

After about six weeks of seeing one another fairly constantly, Henry took me away for a long weekend in the Cotswolds. It was idyllic. He didn't actually ask me to marry him, but he did say that he was really serious about me and hoped I felt the same – of course I did! He then said it was about time I met his family.

It was hopeless right from the beginning – they hated me. I suppose now, looking back on it, I can see why. They didn't need me in their life. They'd managed alone with their father through all the difficult years of growing up, so why should they suddenly now get lumbered with a stepmother?

I asked Henry why he'd never considered marrying before and his answer made sense – he simply hadn't had time. Raising his daughters had taken up every ounce of his energy, and it was only now that he was having time to think about himself. It seemed so unfair that he had devoted himself unselfishly to his children through all those years, and now in return they resented him having any life of his own.

I tried being nice to them, I really did, but they were venomous. They weren't very polite even in front of Henry, but behind his back they were awful. The eldest one, Karen, told me she would do everything she could to stop her father marrying me.

So I gave up. I told Henry I loved him but couldn't cope with his daughters. He begged me to give it time, but I knew it was no good. I knew it would never be right.

The trouble is, I still see him very occasionally, and he told me that he can't help resenting his daughters for what's happened. So, you see, everyone's lost out – Henry and I don't

38

have each other, and I've ruined his relationship with his children. But what else could I have done? I knew I couldn't cope with their bitterness – even Henry wasn't worth that.

Did Betty make the right decision? It's hard to tell. Perhaps time would have changed the children's attitudes. Or perhaps, subconsciously, Henry was actually proud of his daughters' possessiveness of him – maybe it made him feel important and proved in his own mind that he had done a good job. Certainly it didn't sound as though Henry had tried very hard to give Betty any support. If so, and he was not prepared to stand up to his daughters when he was actually trying to woo Betty, there is no chance that things would have improved once they were married. Yet, as Betty says, their failure to make it work has caused unhappiness for everyone. There are no winners in this story.

Be realistic

Perhaps the most important attribute that you can take to prospective step-parenthood is a sense of realism. I see no reason why the average stepchild should like his or her step-parent, or greet their arrival with any enthusiasm. The newcomer is going to dilute the attention they receive from one of their parents. The future marriage will bring to an end all possibility of their parents getting back together again. A step-parent will inevitably change and disrupt their lives.

For this reason, decide as early as possible in this relationship whether you can cope, and then, whatever the decision, stick to it. In all loving relationships you should have a sense of responsibility, and if you are considering taking on the role of a step-parent you need to behave very responsibly indeed. It would be wrong to worry the children unnecessarily if all you expect from their parent is a quick fling before you move on to pastures new.

Don't fall into the trap – or let your partner do so – of imagining that the children fail to understand what is going on. Very young children, and that means three-or four-year-olds, need to be told if this is the lady that Daddy's going to marry. They need everything explained to them – exactly how your growing relationship will affect their lives – in every detail. It is also very helpful for step-parents to spell out what they expect from their relationship with the children. 'I am not your Mummy/Daddy and I am not going to try to be, but I would like to be your friend.' This sort of conversation can come as a huge relief.

Here is a story of a relationship which worked – George and his little brother Jamie live with their mother and grandmother. Their father has fortnightly access on Sundays. George tells the story:

We used to have horrible days out with Dad. We did the same thing every week. He would collect me and Jamie and we would go back to his cottage. Then, no matter what the weather, we'd go for a long walk, all through the woods to the village. And of course we always ended up at the pub.

We had to sit in the children's room while Dad talked to all his friends at the bar. It used to go on and on. We were bored – it was an awful pub, with nothing to do, and Dad always drank too much. We used to ask ourselves why he wanted to see us at all, because he didn't seem to want to spend any time with us, just with his friends. It would get later and later and we'd be hungry, but there was no point in trying to persuade him to leave until the pub shut.

Then we had this long walk home, and Dad would be pretty silly by then because of the drinking. When we got back, sometimes he'd make us lunch, sometimes he'd be too drunk to try and we'd just help ourselves to something. He'd usually open a bottle of wine and sit down in front of the television and fall asleep. When he woke up, it was time for us to go home. There was nothing to do at his house, no games or anything. It was such a waste of Sunday.

Then Dad met Margaret. Me and Jamie didn't like her to start with because she seemed quite fierce. She had two grown-up sons, a lot older than us, who she kept talking about.

Anyway, she started organising our Sundays. We used to go to her house instead of Dad's cottage. We'd still have a big walk before lunch, but not to the pub. Lunch was really good and afterwards we'd do things – go for a bike ride, play croquet, or, if it was bad weather, we'd play card games. Margaret taught us to play chess. Dad didn't drink too much with Margaret around, and he seemed a lot happier.

Mum was upset when they decided to get married, and so me and Jamie wondered if it was a good idea for a while. Now they are married, though, it's really good – we go and stay with them in the holidays sometimes. Margaret's sons are really nice. They take me and Jamie out on treats and they call us their kid brothers – I like that.

It's obvious why this particular second marriage worked for the children. Clearly George and Jamie's Dad needed taking in hand, and Margaret is by all accounts a strong woman. Nothing wrong there, though – strong she may be, but she didn't interfere too much. Father and sons still had their long walks together, and George no longer moaned about them because Margaret made the rest of their day more constructive. The momentary doubt about Dad and Margaret's relationship, caused by their mother's feelings, was understandable – but they seemed to have weathered that and have discovered the advantages of older brothers. Margaret and Dad (despite his boozing!) seem to have handled their relationship very well indeed, so far as George and Jamie are concerned.

It all sounds very tortuous and daunting, doesn't it – this laying down of the foundations for such an important yet unexpected relationship. It is vital to stress that you do not have to adore children in order to be a good step-parent. But you do have to like people and be interested in them. In other words you need to be someone who makes an effort with relationships if you are going to make a real success of step-parenthood. Of course, making a real success may not even be necessary. Your stepchildren may be grown up, or not based with your partner, or very small and heavily involved with the other partner and family.

Whatever the situation, one thing is absolutely certain – you cannot ignore your prospective partner's parenthood. It exists like the nose on his or her face. It has to be taken into account and recognised for its importance in its own right, as well as for its potential effect on your future marriage. Don't expect too much of yourself. Parenthood is a learning process and step-parenthood even more so, for the rules are less well defined. Don't expect instant success, for undoubtedly you will be disappointed. If you can try to see every situation from the child's point of view as well as your own, then you will be making a very creditable start.

4

Setting Up Home Together

The American term for a stepfamily is a 'blended' family. It is such a positive description, suggesting that something has been achieved. The couple have perhaps got together with one of hers and two of his and have created a new baby of theirs – all blended together into a happy, loving family. It is not easy, but it can be done.

Clearly, when children are involved there are two quite different aspects of setting up a home together to consider. There are the emotional adjustments to be made, and the purely practical, physical problems associated with combining two homes into one. Let us look first at the emotional pitfalls.

As explained in Chapter 3, there is no reason to suppose that any of the children concerned will be pleased at the concept of their parent or parents remarrying, or indeed setting up a permanent home with a new partner. Against this rather negative statement, however, one should not overlook the fact that happiness is very infectious. If you and your partner are in love, full of happy thoughts for your future together, your children may be swept along with the tide of this positive feeling. If the children have been through months or even years of parental unhappiness, it may come as a huge relief to see that at least one of their parents thinks life is worth living again.

Here is Peter again, having reconciled himself to the idea of his father getting married again:

> Mum, of course, was dead against Dad remarrying. I think mostly because she was worried about money. Because Sally is a lot younger than Dad, Mum imagined that they would want to have more children. I like the idea of having younger brothers

and sisters, but as far as Mum's concerned she just sees it as money going to someone else, rather than her. I can't help being pleased about it now, mostly because I'm getting on so much better with Dad – he's a completely different person since he met Sally. He used to be very morose and difficult to talk to, but now he's jolly all the time, really fun. He seems sort of younger, somehow. Sally always treats me like I'm her equal. When I'm with Sally and Dad, it's not like I'm a child. It's like there's three of us, all of the same age – and we do some really crazy things, things I could never have imagined my father doing before. When I tried to explain this to Mum, she says Dad can afford to be like that because he doesn't have the responsibility of bringing me up, and that he's just trying to show off to Sally. But I think he's like he is now because he's happy, and that's really nice.

It is vital to maximise this aspect of your relationship. The decision to get together is over, and all the agonising and self-doubts must be put behind you. You are going to set up a home together, to provide a safe and happy haven for you and your partner plus assorted children – his, hers, yours, whatever. You are making a commitment – not to the bad old past, but to the bright new future you see for you and your family. This does not mean that you should take an entirely Mary Poppins view of life – you will probably be short of money, the children may still be deeply traumatised by what has gone before, there may still be court wrangles going on, and any number of other problems. But this is a new beginning, and what you need to convey to the children is that everything from now is up.

Don't expect to change people
One word of caution: frighteningly often, couples marry in the belief that they will be able to change their partner once they are secure inside a permanent relationship. As many men and women have painfully discovered, this simply does not work. If some recurring habit of your prospective partner is infuriating or even

intolerable in the rosy glow of courtship, after a few months of marriage he or she will be driving you crazy. You must accept the person you plan to marry warts and all. Indeed, most irritating characteristics are more likely to deteriorate than improve.

What is very important is that you also apply this thinking to your future stepchildren. This is how Olivia saw the trouble ahead, and took avoiding action.

The moment I accepted Roy's proposal his attitude towards my daughter, Mandy, began to change. He started to criticise the way she looked. She was fifteen at the time and at a very vulnerable age. He said she wore too much make-up and her skirts were too short. He said I should be firmer with her about what time she stayed out until and who she was with, and even suggested that, without him as a steadying influence, Mandy would go off the rails.

I was really angry about this. Mandy's Dad was killed in a car accident before she was even born, and we had managed very well on our own for fifteen years. We have a wonderful relationship – always have. We fight sometimes, because we're quite alike, but we understand each other and are very protective of one another.

I wasn't having this man telling me how my daughter should behave, even if I did love him. Luckily I saw the danger signals and got out. If I hadn't, I think Roy might have destroyed my relationship with my daughter.

Some of my friends think I'm mad, saying Mandy is nearly grown up and, when she is, I'll still be on my own. But I've no regrets – none at all.

As a step-parent there is no point imagining that, once you are all together under the same roof on a permanent basis, things will be different. If you find the children's behaviour and lack of discipline intolerable when you are not living with them twenty-four hours a day, things are certainly not going to get better when you are. If their table manners or noise level are driving you demented when you see them every other weekend, do not assume that once they are living full time under your roof this is something you will be able to stamp out. Yes, of course, you and your partner can introduce house rules once the security of a permanent home and relationship is established, but you cannot expect to change things overnight and to try to do so is madness.

So what is the solution – to correct the children's table manners before you accept their father's marriage proposal? In a way, yes. It is important, particularly with older children, to sit down and talk through what living together will mean and to try and anticipate the likely difficulties, even if those difficulties seem trivial.

You should not expect the discussion to be one-way for, just as you will have concerns, so will the children. They should be encouraged to tell you about your own infuriating ways.

The exchange of views will not necessarily improve the situation, but it will at least get you talking and may well demonstrate that a high degree of tolerance will be required by everyone. Certainly you should not imagine that getting together under one roof is going to solve anything. It is far more likely to highlight the difficulties than reduce them, at any rate initially. Pat's story illustrates this point:

Eddie and I met through our children. They were not particular friends – it was just that my daughter, Joanna, is in the same year as Eddie's Sam, and because of this we kept on bumping into each other at school functions. Eventually we discovered that we were both single parents and divorced. Eddie's wife had run off with a colleague from work and left Sam to be cared for by his father. It wasn't easy, but he was coping.

We started to go out together. I learned that Eddie had been married twice before and had a seventeen-year-old son called Joseph, who had always lived with his mother.

We fell in love in a matter of a few days. My friends were very sceptical – they said there had to be something wrong with a man who had been married twice before. But from the start I was sure Eddie was right for me.

When we told the children that we were planning to get married they were really pleased – in fact they thought it was quite a laugh. I sold my flat and Joanna and I moved in with Eddie and Sam, just three months after we first met. We married straightaway, for the sake of the children as much as anything, and settled down together just as if it had always been meant to be. All four of us were thrilled with our new family.

We'd been together for about three weeks when Eddie took a phone call one night from Joseph, who said he'd like to come and see us. I was a little nervous. I'd met him briefly at the wedding, where he'd seemed rather an aloof boy and obviously very clever.

He came to stay for the weekend, and on the second day asked whether he could come and live with us. He explained that he felt he'd never had a family life, his mother was a very difficult woman, and he wanted to join our family – at any rate for a year until he went to university. Eddie, of course, was over the moon, and I have to admit that I was flattered. Of course we said yes.

It didn't really work from the very beginning. Joseph would do nothing to help. He'd been used to being waited on hand and foot by his mother, and when I asked him to clear the table or fetch the coal he simply refused or said he'd do it in a while – and then never did. He seemed to think that there was one rule for the younger children and one for him, which, of course, was true up to a point.

However, he seemed to enjoy flaunting his behaviour, which was unsettling for Sam and Joanna. They could see that Joseph got away with things, and so began to think it was clever to defy me. Eddie missed a lot of this, of course, being at work. He thought I was exaggerating.

Things came to a head one day – it was over such a stupid thing. I asked Joseph to help me unload some heavy shopping from the car and he refused point blank, saying he was too busy. I just told him to get on and do it.

He rounded on me and said he would not be ordered around in his father's house. I realised in that moment that he saw us simply as visitors in his father's house – not just me and

Joanna but Sam, too, who after all was only his half-brother. I was so shocked that I unloaded the shopping alone.

Afterwards I began to re-examine his motives for wanting to come and live with us, and I began to see that what he was really trying to do was to establish his superiority in his relationship with his father. It wasn't that he wanted to be part of our family. He was testing his father to see if with a new wife and stepchild there was still a place for him.

On the one hand this made me feel very sorry for him because I could see how insecure he was, despite the fact that he was nearly a man. On the other hand I was infuriated. We had been such a happy little family and now, thanks to Joseph, things were falling apart.

Eddie was very good, very supportive. After the shopping incident things deteriorated rapidly, and got to such a pitch that in the end he told Joseph that he would have to go – and he went. He visits us occasionally. He doesn't live with his mother now – he's at university and I think doing very well. He seems happy, and just in the last few months it seems he has a regular girlfriend.

I still have a sense of failure, though. He's polite enough to me now, but very distant, and I know he bears a grudge. I wonder whether if it had been my home that Eddie and Sam had moved into it would have made any difference. We'll never know, but I feel guilty and I know Eddie does, too.

The crunch point of this story seems to be when Joseph 'pulled rank' and referred to the family home as his father's house. Maybe it is wrong to place too much emphasis on this, but it certainly struck a chord with Pat. Children are always looking for ways to put their parents ahead of their step-parents – to find a way of keeping their step-parents in their place. Arguably, one could say that in order for a step-parent to have equal status within the home the family house needs to be jointly owned by parent and step-parent.

New relationship, new home

This brings us to the practical aspects of setting up home together. If humanly possible, two people getting together for the first time with any variety of children should start again. In other words, she should not move in with him or he with her – they should buy or rent a new home. There can be few more difficult situations to handle than a step-parent moving into a house which has formerly been lived in by both natural parents. This is a potential nightmare for the step-parent and, indeed, for the children. The step-parent entering the former family home cannot help but feel an intruder. Of course, the situation is unavoidable, particularly in today's difficult property climate, but do try to make alternative arrangements.

This is the story of Gemma, now well into her sixties. A long time ago she married a man called Andrew, whose first wife had left him for another man. Andrew was nearly thirty years older than Gemma, and you would have thought he would have done anything to make his new, extremely pretty young wife happy.

When I moved in it seemed as if Mary, his ex-wife, was every-where. In those days, because she had run off with another man she was denied custody of the children. So Mary and Andrew's two children, who were then five and seven, lived with us. There was a full-time housekeeper to look after us all, so I was let in gently when it came to learning to care for the children.

They were not a problem except that, just like everything else, they were Mary's – there was Mary's desk in the morning room, Mary's chair by the fire. . . . Do you know, her photo-graph was still by his bed and some of her clothes still in the wardrobe? No one had even thought to take them out when I arrived. The housekeeper, Mrs Bennett, was an old bitch and hated me, so I suppose she had left everything there on pur-pose. But one would have thought that Andrew would have used a little imagination.

The first years were hell – I seemed to be living in Mary's

shadow all the time. After a while I began to realise what it was – Andrew had been something of a stud in his youth, and he just couldn't bear the idea of his wife leaving him for someone else. By leaving so much of Mary in the house he could pretend it hadn't happened. It sounds peculiar, but I'm sure that's how his mind worked. Even so, understanding the situation didn't make it easier.

I gave him two more children, but even they didn't make me feel on an equal footing with Mary. His and Mary's children became fond of me – they practically never saw their mother – and to all the world we were a very happy family. But I still felt I was living in Mary's house, living Mary's life.

By the time I met her we were both fairly elderly – I in my early sixties, she in her seventies. It was strange. She was nothing like how I had imagined – a very kind, open, warm person and not the cold-hearted bitch I'd always believed her to be. I would have explained to her how I felt, but by then, you see, it wasn't relevant – for the first time we met was at Andrew's funeral.

If there is no alternative to living in the former family home, then drastic steps must be taken to change certain aspects of the house. The most emotive and important place is the bedroom. No sensible parent will invite a new partner to share the room, and perhaps even the bed, that he once shared with his children's other parent. Even if the new couple end up with the smallest bedroom in the house, there must be a shift round to make sure that this situation cannot arise.

A swop of rooms will inevitably mean that one or more children will have to change their rooms, too. However, bearing in mind that in most cases this will mean a move to the biggest bedroom, it is unlikely that there will be too much fuss – particularly if a little bribery in the form of new decorations and curtains is thrown in. Even quite young children will appreciate what is happening. There is something definitely wrong about keeping the status quo, and children are very prudish.

So far as the rest of the house is concerned, here again considerable tact is needed. If, before the marriage broke up, Father used to work from home in a little office off the kitchen, it would be foolish for the new stepfather to think, 'Oh, good, I've always wanted a study,' and move in. Far better to offer this little room as a bedroom to one of the children. Who knows, if they are missing their Dad they might welcome this opportunity to have his old room.

This applies to any room which has been particularly personal to the missing parent – perhaps Mother had a little room where she used to do the sewing and ironing and where the children came for a cosy chat. Perhaps Dad's greenhouse at the bottom of the garden is also the place where he used to slope off with his coffee and newspaper and where the children could be sure of finding him if they wanted to have a natter. Sensitivity over these apparently small issues is vital. So if, for financial or practical reasons, there is no alternative to the step-parent moving into the former marital home, then just remember you are treading on eggshells.

Blending personalities and lifestyles

The situation is less disaster-prone if one partner moves into the other's house when it has no connection with the former marriage. Tact is still required, but the whole situation is far less emotive. This is what happened when my husband, Alan, and I got together:

When Alan and I decided to get married, he had been on his own for several years. He had bought and converted an old school house in a village. He is by nature a very neat and tidy person – I think it comes from being an accountant! Living alone in what to all intents and purposes was a brand-new house had intensified this side of his nature. The house was always terrifyingly immaculate – the cushions plumped, the washing-up done and the carpets vacuumed.

By contrast my five-year-old daughter Lucy and I lived in semi-controlled chaos in a little Victorian terraced house some twenty miles away. I am not naturally a tidy person, and at the time I was running my own business as well as being a single parent, so the finer domestic details tended to get overlooked. We shared our house with a scruffy mongrel and a Burmese cat – which is more monkey than cat and spends a great deal of time clawing its way up curtains and demolishing furniture.

You can imagine how the panic set in at Alan's suggestion that Lucy and I should move into his house. I could not see how my family could possibly move into Alan's meticulous home without driving him mad. We discussed the problem, and solved it by putting up a permanent staircase to the attic space. There were two rooms up there, one of which we turned into a bedroom for Lucy while the other became my study/work-room and Lucy's playroom.

On Christmas Eve I, Lucy, the dog and, as it turned out, the newly pregnant cat moved in – to the attic! All our mess was contained there, and at first when we tentatively came down-stairs we were on our best behaviour. It worked like a charm – the shock to Alan's system was minimal, and we rather began to like living in a clean, tidy atmosphere. We merged or 'blended', as our American friends would say. Gradually, like some ghastly disease, our mess crept down the attic stairs, but it was a more controlled mess than hitherto.

Now, eleven years later and two babies later, we have a for-mula, a sort of compromise which is acceptable to us both. And Alan still has the safe haven of his office, into which none of us may enter without invitation!

I appreciate that we were lucky. At the time we had both the space and the money to make our transition into communal living as trauma-free as possible. But not everyone is faced with the differences of personality that Alan and I were. The important aspect to consider, whatever your circumstances, is how each partner, and associated children, like to live, or are used to living, and to recognise that, even though they are leaving their home, they must be allowed to take some vestiges of their former lifestyle with them.

Although I was desperately happy about marrying

Alan, I do remember shedding a tear on leaving our old home. It was the first house I had ever been able to call my own, and Lucy and I had been happy there. We were giving up a way of life that would never come back. It was the end of an era – goodbye to Lucy's babyhood, goodbye, up to a point, to the intimacy we had shared as child and single parent living alone.

Much is made in this book of the need to consider children's feelings – but don't forget to consider your own and those of your partner too. Even if your way of life has not been particularly agreeable, it is what you have been used to. No major change in your life can ever be made without glancing over your shoulder at what went before. When that change also involves someone else's children, certainly new step-parents with no children of their own will find themselves glancing over their shoulder – not only are the carefree single days over, but so are the childless ones. It is a big step.

And so we come on to the ideal. If at all possible, you, your partner and children should go house-hunting together. If the children are over the age of three you should involve them in the process as much as possible – looking at estate agents' details, viewing houses, planning whose room will be whose, what colour the walls are decorated and so on. That way, long before you move into the new house it will feel like everyone's home, because everyone has played a part in the decision-making. It is the happiest and best way to start out on a new family life, as Janet found:

I'm so glad Paul and I decided to buy a new house when we got together. We did it for practical reasons – I had three children living permanently with me, and Paul had two who visited regularly. We both love children and wanted to have one or two more together. Catering for up to seven children meant we certainly needed a bigger place then either of us lived in. So we put our properties on the market and started house-hunting.

It was only when we were doing it that we both suddenly

53

realised that the experience was a great deal more valuable than simply finding a big enough roof under which to house everyone. The children joined in with real enthusiasm, and when we eventually found the right place they simply took over – planned where everybody should sleep and where the climbing frame and swing should go, and where the sand pit should be built and all that sort of thing. What was particularly lovely was that my daughter, Claire, and Paul's daughter, Lynn, decided to share a room. Of course for part of the time Lynn isn't there, but that's not the point – even before we were married and living together they saw themselves as sisters.

I have to say it's worked out splendidly. The children really are one big, happy family and I think our new home has a lot to do with it. I'm just so terribly grateful we made the decision we did.

Familiarity means security

A word of caution, though, over new homes: in an effort to project the glories of the new, don't forget the importance of the old. My own daughter had five different homes before her fourth birthday, and I became a dab hand at creating essentially the same bedroom in whatever house we happened to live – ranging from a flat over the garage to a fourteenth-century cottage. The same curtains would be let up and down, the same pictures hung on the wall, and the cot was always put in the same place relative to the window and door. I always splashed the same peachy-coloured paint on the walls.

Of course, what applies to a baby or very young child does not necessarily apply to an older child. None the less, possessions are very important to children – particularly children who have had much that was familiar taken from their lives. You may feel that your stepson is too old for Paddington Bear curtains, and you have seen some lovely material in a local shop printed with vintage cars or aeroplanes. Be very wary. He may need his Paddington Bear curtains for another few months. Take your lead from him. Even teenage children may wish to re-create their old room in the new house – in which case let them, for they clearly need the security.

Moving experiences

The same rules that you would apply to children moving in any circumstances apply when a new family get together. Because of the crazy way in which houses are bought and sold, one cannot choose precisely when one moves. If it is during the school term, teachers need to be alerted. Unless they are in the middle of important exams, children should ideally have a few days off to settle in. If the move also means a new school, children need first to get used to the new home before the new school is attempted. You may long for them to be out from under your feet during the day so that you can sort out the house, but don't rush this stage. The adjustments they are being expected to make are too great: they must deal with them one at a time. This was Fran's unhappy experience of the time:

> When Steven and I got married we recognised that my twin boys, George and Henry, then aged seven, had a lot of adjusting to do. Not only did they have to get used to having a stepfather but we also moved house, feeling it was not right to live either in our old home or Steven's. The trouble was, the only place we could afford was in a different school catchment area, so it meant that the boys had to start at a new school as well.
>
> Within a few days it became obvious that Henry was not happy. I talked to George about it, but he had no idea what was wrong and Henry wouldn't tell him.
>
> The boys are non-identical twins and very different in both looks and temperament – George is the physical one and also the outgoing, popular one. Henry has always been smaller and shy, and he also loved his old home and school. He seemed to be shrinking before our very eyes – moping and quiet, not rude or angry, just heartbroken. George told us that his brother was being bullied at school, but we felt it was a symptom rather than the cause of what was wrong with him.

In the end we became so worried about him – he was very pale and thin – that I took him to the doctor, who referred us to a psychiatrist. I don't know what the psychiatrist said to him, because she talked to him alone. But when she saw Steven and me afterwards she seemed quite convinced that Henry's problems stemmed from there being too many changes in his life at once. He was just overwhelmed by what had happened to him. He was clearly pining for his old way of life – his old home, his old friends and his old school. The psychiatrist was sure that he was idealising all these aspects of his former life, far beyond the reality of how they had actually been. It was just his way of coping with all the changes.

Steven asked whether it would help if we moved back to the area where we had come from. The psychiatrist asked Steven if he really meant it, and he said yes, he did. She said, 'Try the idea out on Henry. You may be surprised by the result.'

That evening we sat down with both boys and suggested to Henry that perhaps it might be best if we moved back to our original home town and he went back to his old school. Obviously we'd have to find a different house, but we thought we would be able to find one relatively nearby.

George seemed genuinely disappointed, but was quite tactful about his feelings. Henry seemed gob-smacked – absolutely astounded that we should consider taking such drastic action on his behalf. He said he would like to think about it, and the following morning, almost casually over breakfast, he said no, he'd like to stay where he was.

We were, as the psychiatrist had suggested, extremely surprised by his decision. We'd assumed he would jump at the chance. With sinking hearts, we were already contemplating another move. It was fascinating, though. From that day Henry perked up. In other words, the moment we gave him the opportunity to go back he was somehow released from his sadness and was able to look to the future.

I would tell anyone making such radical changes in a child's life that they should be very aware of the sort of child they are dealing with. In George's case it was no problem. In Henry's I believe it could have caused disastrous long-term problems.

Status, space and fitting everyone in

So far this chapter has assumed that, as a step-parent, you are inheriting your partner's children. But you may also be a parent yourself, about to bring together several children, including your own, under one roof. Let's consider the practical aspects of housing more than one child of possibly differing status (for more detail on siblings, see Chapter 6). In other words, as a stepmother for example, you may have your own children living with you but your new husband's children may only visit occasionally. The question is, how do you house everyone?

It would be unrealistic in these circumstances to allocate a bedroom per child, whether that child is living permanently in the family or just visiting. However, visiting children who have no permanent space will always tend to feel that they are visitors. And there can be huge resentment on the part of the resident children if the arrival of visitors means they have to move out of their bedrooms or share with another child whom they hardly know. Some parents manage a complicated juggling act whereby the resident children visit their other parent when the visiting children come to stay. This may seem like a very neat solution, but it isn't perfect. Of course if the two sets of children don't get on well it is a possible answer, but it has the effect of fragmenting the family. Lizzie thought she was doing the best for everybody, but discovered that she was, in fact exacerbating the situation.

> My two girls, and Bob's daughter, Janet, appeared not to like each other from the very beginning, although they were much of an age. We obviously introduced them very early on, before we even decided to get married. They seemed to be deeply resentful of one another, and at our wedding it was disastrous – all three were bridesmaids and clearly loathed one another.
>
> For that reason, once we were married we tended to keep them apart. My two lived with us permanently, visiting their father only occasionally, and Janet did not seem over-anxious

to visit us – her permanent home, too, was with her mother. We arranged that when Janet came for the weekend, my two went to see their father. The theory was good – it enabled us to concentrate our time on Janet when she was with us and avoided, as we thought, any sort of problems.

It took a while before the resentment started coming out. My elder daughter, Rebecca, asked one day why it was that Janet always came when they were away – 'I suppose it's because she hates us,' said Rebecca. Janet in turn asked why it was that Rebecca and her sister were never there when she came. In other words, there was interest in one another.

So, taking a deep breath, one weekend Bob and I arranged for them all to be at home. It was extraordinary – before the first day was out they were firm friends, and have been ever since. It would never occur to us now to send the girls off when Janet is due for a weekend – she would have a miserable time without them.

Janet is also much more anxious to visit us now. We consider the girls' initial reaction not at all surprising – the poor children suddenly had stepsisters foisted upon them. Maybe we should have been more sensitive of their feelings – or maybe it was just a stage they had to go through.

There are ways in which you can tactfully handle an invasion of children. From the resident children's point of view, maybe they can have a spare bed in their room which can be used for friends as well as visiting stepbrothers and stepsisters. If the visitor is a regular one, the room can be naturally divided with a curtain or bookshelves to give each child some privacy.

If the visiting child cannot have a permanent bedroom 'to come home to', there are alternatives. A shelf, or a toy box, or a couple of drawers which are exclusively his or hers can go a long way towards creating a sense of belonging. This can be extended – how about the whole family having mugs with their names on, including those of the visiting stepchildren? The same could apply to napkin rings. How about permanent toothbrushes, or personalised hooks on the bathroom door for dressing gowns or towels? It is these little things which make such a difference.

If, say, you are normally a family of four, but every so often your partner's children visit, it involves very little outlay to make the house feel, from the visiting children's point of view, as though it is really a home for six people. Parents can be so tactless; for instance, the visiting children may be given different cutlery or crockery from the rest of the family, indicating that there is not enough of the family's normal tableware to go round. This instantly creates the feeling of being different.

So when planning your new home, right from the beginning include the visitors as well as the permanent residents. However, be careful not to do this in a pressurising way – it could be dangerous to make a child, whose main home is with someone else, feel over-catered for in his visiting home. If, for example, you create a palatial bedroom for him which is far bigger and better than the one in which he sleeps normally, you will be doing him no favours at all. Striking a balance is the thing – creating a home where everyone has a place and feels welcome, secure, whether it is their permanent or part-time home.

Holidays bring people together

One final point on homemaking – before you set up home together, you, your partner and associated children should try to get away on holiday. It does not need to be anywhere very exotic – just a chance to be together in some place where to the outside world you will simply be an ordinary family like anyone else. You will all learn so much about one another, particularly about the practical aspects. You might discover, for instance, that five-year-old Tom is a light sleeper – therefore it would be silly to put him in the room over the kitchen, where the family tends to spend their evenings. His older sister Mary and your daughter Elizabeth might get on so well on holiday that you consider talking them into sharing a room together after all – that sort of thing.

Holidays are very good for family unity. The family finds itself in a strange environment and automatically turns inwards, seeking protection and comfort from one another. This certainly proved to be so in our own family's case:

Alan and I adopted a little boy from Romania two years ago. After a very difficult winter when we had all caught flu from each other, we took the whole family away in early spring to Cornwall to recuperate. It was the turning point. Although Michael had settled into the family wonderfully well and we all adored him, the holiday somehow cemented us as a family although we were only away for a week.

What, in this instance, applies to an adopted child equally well applies to a stepchild. We tend to see ourselves as others see us, and in a funny way being perceived by the world as a united family tends to make one feel just that.

5

The Wider Family

When you get married, whatever the circumstances, you will invariably find that a great deal more is involved than simply loving your chosen partner – there are mothers-in-law and sisters-in-law, aunts, uncles, grannies and cousins, all of whom have an apparent vested interest in your relationship. This new family will have views on how you look, where you live, your job prospects, your likelihood of making a success of the marriage, when and if you should have children, and so on. Most of us have at some stage in our life been paraded before a set of in-laws for the first time, and there can be few experiences more daunting.

Trial by in-laws
It is reasonable to assume that the situation will be worse if you join the family as a second husband or wife – or third or fourth, come to that! Inevitably you will be compared with your predecessor in every minute detail. If you have the misfortune to be considered responsible for the former marriage breaking up, your chances of acceptability among your in-laws are slender. You may well be considered a Jezebel or a cad, according to gender, even if they know that the previous marriage was not happy. The general feeling will be that it is hardly worth making your acquaintance because you will be off in a minute to wreck another marriage.

Consider, therefore, how much more complex the whole situation becomes if there are children from the previous marriage to consider. Now you will be judged on your suitability not only as a husband or wife but as a step-parent. The extended family will be particularly disapproving of a marriage break-up where children are concerned, which is understandable, and you will have to work very hard indeed to gain acceptance into the inner circle. Margery was only twenty when she had to cope with her future in-laws' disapproval.

I will never forget my first introduction to my husband's family. They were all there – his widowed mother, his mother's sister who was terrifying, and then a huge array of uncles, aunts and cousins. Ostensibly they were all getting together because it was the great-aunt's seventy-fifth birthday. But, at the risk of sounding paranoid, I knew that they were really there to have a look at me.

Ken's marriage to his former wife had been unhappy for years, but he had done nothing about it until he met me. So I was the 'marriage-wrecker' and the 'wicked stepmother' to Ken's children.

Their questions were so bitchy and pointed. Ken's mother asked me if I'd dyed my hair. His aunt assumed I bought ready-made food and stuck it in the microwave. I'm not a bad cook, and I was really offended. They suggested that it must be a great shock to the system having Ken's children to stay with us from time to time – by insinuation they were suggesting I would never be able to cope. They even dismissed my job as trivial. It was horrible, the whole thing.

Ken was marvellous and never left my side. The following day, rather like after the first night of a West End play, we waited for the reviews.

Strangely enough, it was Ken's terrifying aunt who rang first and said I was 'a surprisingly nice little thing', and should make a good addition to the family. The thaw had set in! Ken and I now have two children of our own and our sons have finally ensured my acceptance – I couldn't be made to feel more welcome. I've vowed, though, to be very sympathetic to my daughters-in-law, right from the start!

In addition to your partner's family, you may also be faced with the step-in-laws – in other words, your partner's former partner's family – the other grandparents of your stepchildren. Let's face it, there is no reason why they should like you. Whatever the circumstances, even if you played no part in the breaking up of the marriage, you have taken over the role which once belonged exclusively to their child. Even if they are glad their child has divorced your partner, they will still resent you, particularly if you appear to be both pleasant and happy. This is a classic 'no win' situation. If your relationship does not work out, then you will have failed and caused their grandchildren yet more disruption. If your relationship succeeds, it is a direct slur on their own child!

If you do get on with all the different family elements, make sure they don't get too intrusive. In an effort to be fair to everyone you can feel you are being pulled apart when what is most important is the family nucleus. You, your partner and the children must come first. As with everything else, a balancing act is involved – keeping the relationships going, but not to the detriment of the family as a whole. Eventually Lucinda realised that this is how things had to be:

It got stupid, to the point where we never had a free moment to ourselves. With three children between us, from two different marriages, we were expected to socialise with a vast circle of people – Thomas's parents, Thomas's former wife's parents, Thomas's wife's new children, my parents, my ex-husband's parents, an ex-husband's brother's family, my brother's family, my grandmother and great-aunt.

The children all lived with us, but living was hardly the word to describe it. They boarded with us during the week, which with GCSEs approaching meant they were knee-deep in either homework or television, or, all too often, both! Come the weekend, however, we were all spirited off somewhere or forced to entertain out of sheer guilt.

In the end we had a family conference and found the children felt exactly the same as we did. So we announced that we were going to be hermits, using the excuse of school exams, and saw no one from the family for a couple of months. It was absolute bliss and, although we're now being more sociable again, it's on a very limited basis. We have to come first – we are a family in our own right, not a collection of public property.

Let's look now at the various relationships within the extended family which you are likely to meet.

The other 'other half'

If children are involved, you are likely to have some kind of contact with your partner's former husband or wife. Although you may wish to keep this to an absolute minimum it is important that you can at least talk to one another, if for no other reason than that you might need to do so in a crisis. Women tend to be better at handling this complex relationship than men, who feel threatened by the other man in their wife's life; women, on the other hand, are more practical and down to earth and usually have more moral courage.

Having said that, while most women can forgive another woman for 'stealing' their husband, they can never forgive that woman for 'stealing' their child. In a good parental relationship the natural mother has an overwhelming desire to protect and nurture her child – never more so than when that child is hurt and traumatised by a marriage break-up. A stepmother will almost certainly be seen as a threat by the natural mother; while this equally applies to fathers and stepfathers, it is not likely to be so powerful an emotion.

Children are only too aware of their parents' (and step-parents') vulnerability and will shamelessly play it for all its worth. 'Janie makes much better spaghetti bolognese than you do, Mum,' says her ten-year-old little horror on returning from a visit to Dad and his new stepmum. The child enjoys a sense of power at seeing his mother's agitation, yet he cannot begin to understand the pain he is causing. When his mother learns that his stepmother's spaghetti bolognese is better than her own, she subconsciously fears that her son will leave home and go and live with his father and step-mother, and that she will lose him for ever. The fact that deep down she knows he is very happy where he is, that he is settled in his school and with his local friends, makes no difference, for she cannot see the situation impartially. Her inferior spaghetti bolognese has her life in ruins.

As a step-parent it is vital that you understand the depth of emotion, pain, hurt and jealousy that you can cause the natural parent you have replaced in your part-ner's life. When a child is born, most loving parents feel a sense of inadequacy and a desperate desire to try and make the world a perfect place for their growing baby. Whatever the parents do in the years ahead, they will always be plagued with doubts as to whether they have really acted in their child's best interests or whether his or her problems, however small, are their fault.

The break-up of their marriage, loving parents are quick to realise, is the ultimate betrayal of their chil-dren. The natural seeds of guilt and inadequacy are blown up out of all proportion. They are forever feeling that they should be making it up to their children for all the pain they have caused them. Understanding this will in turn help you to recognise why many divorced par-ents appear over-indulgent with their children. Take Lizzie's story:

When we married, Julian and I didn't expect things to be easy. I had two girls of seven and nine from my previous marriage, and Julian had a girl and a boy from his, who were then eight and twelve. My girls live with us permanently – their father has emigrated to New Zealand and has started a new life. Julian's children visit us for an occasional weekend and for about a week in each of the school holidays.

I genuinely believed when we married that we had sorted out all the likely problems we would encounter with the chil-dren. I thought we had been very realistic in not expecting too much harmony too soon, but I had not anticipated Julian's behaviour. He is quite hard on my girls – makes them sit through meals, expects them to do a lot of chores around the house, and is very keen on good manners. At first I didn't mind all this – in fact I thought it was good for them to have a more structured life, as their father has been so very casual.

However, what I can't bear is the contrast in his behaviour towards his own children. When they come to stay, it's like a visitation from the Queen – everything has to be just so, perfect, and if that isn't bad enough their mother rings up every five minutes to check that all is going well. We're all on tenterhooks, we're so tense.

Julian's children behave abominably the whole time. He has two completely different sets of rules for my children and his. I've tackled him about it, of course, but he says because he sees his children so rarely he doesn't want to spoil things by being too hard on them.

Basically he's in a blind panic all the time that he's going to lose contact with them. The children sense this, and use it unmercifully. His son, David, told Julian on his last visit that his mother was thinking of stopping the visits because he and his sister found them too upsetting. It was just a deliberate ploy to wind up his father – it made me furious, because I could see through it immediately, but not Julian, oh no.

I don't know where we go from here. The resentment gets worse and worse, and of course my girls can't help but feel resentful, too. It's an impossible situation.

This story conveys perfectly the natural parent's nervousness. The mother is clearly terrified that the children have too good a time with their father, so she rings them constantly and issues threats about discontinuing the visits. The father is equally nervous that his wife may try and discontinue the visits, and so falls over backwards to over-indulge his children. The result is that nobody feels happy, secure or relaxed.

It may be asking a lot, but the only person who can really do anything in this situation is Lizzie. If she could forget for one moment the hurt she feels on behalf of her daughters, and try and look dispassionately at the situation, she might be able to get both parents together and explain to them how much they are hurting both each other and the children. If she could explain to the mother that she has two children of her own and doesn't want to take on her children full-time as well, the mother would feel hugely reassured. The mother might then be able to admit to Julian that a break from the children now and again is a blessed relief, and he in turn would feel reassured. Everybody could then relax. As it is, nothing will improve the situation unless somebody can act as the catalyst – the parents are too close to the problem.

Earlier I mentioned how important it is to be a good communicator if you are to be a successful step-parent. While you do not want to turn family life into a series of analytical discussions, you do need to get on with people; and one of the best recipes for successful step-parenthood and remarriage is to form some sort of relationship, however tenuous, with your partner's ex. Children will feel enormous relief. There will have been enough scrapping and squabbling in their lives, and it is so much more practical, too, if the two wives can ring each other up without embarrassment and awkwardness to discuss clothes, holidays, deliveries and collections.

However, it needs to be recognised that the initiative to set up this kind of relationship may well have to come from you, the step-parent. The breakthrough will come when you can convince the natural parent that you are not trying to take over her role, that you do not resent your husband's maintenance obligations, and, above all, that you should not be considered as the enemy – you are both on the same side: the side of the children. That may seem a tall order, but it is achievable. Maggie has a fascinating story to tell:

When Robert and I got together, I was very nervous of his ex-wife, Hilary. She is ten years older than me and seemed very formidable and self-assured. I was a terrible cook – well, I was only twenty-two – and she was brilliant. She was something very high-powered in advertising, while I was a lowly audio-typist. She made me feel thoroughly inadequate and so did her two sons, who clearly thought I was a very poor substitute for their talented mother.

The years went by, and we saw her occasionally when the boys came to visit. I had two children of my own, and it was then that Robert started messing about seriously. I knew, or rather suspected, that he'd had one or two affairs before, but when I was knee-deep in nappies and tired all the time it was all too obvious that he had someone else. We started having terrible rows – we had money problems too – and he had just stalked out of the house one day when Hilary rang up to talk about one of the boys' school outings. I suppose she could tell from my voice that something was wrong, and before I knew where I was I had agreed that she could come round and see me.

When she arrived she sort of took over. She sent her boys upstairs to look after my two, poured us both stiff drinks and suggested I told her everything, which I did. She was wonderful, such a comfort, because she'd been there herself and knew exactly what it felt like. She made me see it was not the end of the world, that I had choices – to stay with Robert and put up with his philandering, or start a life of my own.

I decided to give it another try, and Hilary rang me up regularly: she was really supportive. But when at last, about eighteen months later, I decided I'd had enough, she really came into her own – helping me find somewhere to live, and organising childcare for the children so that I could work a little.

My mother was rather sceptical about Hilary's help. She suggested that maybe she wanted Robert and me to break up to prove that she, too, had done the right thing. However, I am sure it wasn't that, because in the beginning she had backed my decision to try and stay with him.

We really are best friends now, and we can laugh about Robert and his adventures. He hasn't married again – we suspect because he can't bear the thought of any more ex-wives ganging up on him. Our friendship is a very positive thing. We don't moan about the past or even talk about Robert much. It's lovely for the children, though – my two love their big half-

brothers and the feeling is mutual. Crazy, isn't it, to think that
Hilary is my best friend?

The story of Maggie and Hilary is very heartening:
while it might be more conventional to hate your partner's ex, it is not necessary and certainly not desirable.
People often marry and form relationships with the
same type of person, in both looks and character, so it is
quite conceivable that you might actually like the former man or woman in your partner's life. Why keep the
relationship at arm's length? Why not be friends? It
would be marvellous for the children.

Grandparents: pros and cons

As far as parents are concerned, grandparents can be the
world's best natural resource. They are usually fantas-
tic, particularly with small children and have so much
to offer, in many instances that most prized of all possessions – time. Of course, today grandparents often
lead very active lives. If not actually working, they are
almost certainly not confined to their rocking chairs!
Nonetheless their value is immense, and a good relationship between grandparents and grandchildren is of
enormous benefit to the whole family.

If grandparents already play an important role in the
life of your stepchildren, respect and nurture the relationship. Important in any family, grandparents are
much more vital to the child damaged by separation
and divorce, for they represent continuity. Mummy and
Daddy may have split up, maybe the children are living
somewhere new, maybe there are step-parents and new
babies to cope with; but Granny and Grandpa are still
there, living in the same place, doing the same things
day in, day out, gloriously reassuring and absolute balm
to the soul of the traumatised child. Philippa learnt a
useful lesson as to the value of grandparents.

When Gerald and I split up we were at our wits' end as to what
to do with Tiffany. We thought at sixteen she would be largely

unaffected by our divorce – after all, she was on the threshold of her own adult life. Quite the contrary – she seemed to take it worse than a lot of our friends' children who were years younger.

We were shocked and totally unprepared for this reaction. She was moody and depressed and kept going into violent rages. We both had someone new in our lives. Really there wasn't that degree of animosity between us, so we thought she'd be quite accepting of the situation. It wasn't as though there was some terrifically injured party with Gerald and I slanging away at each other.

At sixteen, the question of custody didn't really arise. We simply said to Tiffany that she could live with whichever one of us she wished. She was simply awful with the new man in my life, Martin, and said that if we started living together permanently she would never live with me again. She was not much better with Gerald's new woman, Judy.

Meanwhile we were trying to conduct a civilised divorce, and the whole situation was becoming impossible. It was years since Gerald and I had been united over anything, but we both agreed our daughter was behaving like a spoilt brat. Then one day she came down for breakfast with a sunny smile on her face and said, 'I'm going to live with Granny.'

I was appalled. My mother is well on the wrong side of seventy and very straitlaced. Tiffany is stunning to look at, has scores of boyfriends and was just embarking on a course at art college. I could see no way that it could work out. I said as much, which caused another row, and when I phoned Gerald about it he absolutely agreed, saying he wouldn't give it three days.

I tried to explain to my mother that it wouldn't work, but she was adamant that it would be fine. She said they had always been close, which was true, but of course she was thinking of the child, not the teenager.

All this happened two years ago, and I have to admit that we were wrong. It has been the best possible thing for both of them. It has given my mother a new lease of life, and it has given Tiffany the security she apparently needed.

Looking back on it, with her father and me working

throughout her childhood, I suppose my mother has been the mainstay of her life. I just couldn't see it – I couldn't see how this trendy teenager and this old lady mentally stuck in the thirties could possibly live together. Anyway it's worked, and I'm deeply grateful.

But it does not stop there – you must acknowledge the importance of both sets of grandparents. This may present a very difficult situation, but for the sake of the children you must try and keep the relationships going.

Against this, of course, old people do enjoy meddling – you must not allow yourself to be manipulated. If you and your partner have got together and formed a new family, it may no longer be appropriate for the children to go and spend Christmas Day with their maternal or paternal grandparents. New rituals may need to be established.

It is also worth mentioning that children's relationships with their grandparents should not be all take. As they get older, their grandparents' behaviour may start to irritate – maybe Granny is a bit pernickety and Grandpa tells the same stories over and over again, boring everyone to tears. None the less, if grandparents enjoy their grandchildren's company it is good for the younger members of the family, including teenagers, to spend some time with them.

While talking of grandparents, stepgrandparents must not be overlooked. Your own parents could well have a vital role to play in the success of your new family. If you do not have children of your own, their first experience of grandparenthood may be their stepgrandchildren. They might be absolutely thrilled to acquire a ready-made family, in which case you should encourage this relationship for all it's worth! The forming of a good relationship between your stepchildren and your parents is all part of the blending process, making everyone feel more secure and settled in the new arrangement. Everyone loves attention, and the children will be flattered by your parents' desire to make them feel part of their family too.

However, with three possible sets of interested grandparents, competition can develop, which must at all costs be avoided as it can bring extra pressure to bear on the children. They have enough to cope with without warring wrinklies! Marian's story demonstrates the point:

His mother very nearly broke up our marriage. Michael and I met and married very quickly, but I was no part of his marriage breakdown – he was already living separately from his wife when we met. My mother-in-law, however, refused to accept this, although she must have known it was true.

Very early on in our marriage I learned that she had told Michael's three children that I had been responsible for the marriage break-up. We only found out because Elizabeth, Michael's eldest child, was so upset by what her grandmother had said about me that she talked it through with him. Of course he told her it wasn't true, but the damage had been done.

The children, aged five to nine, spent part of every holiday with us and, but for their grandmother's bitching, we got on really well. As it was, though, they did seem deeply suspicious of me and, in fairness to Michael's ex-wife, we were both sure that it was nothing to do with her.

Playing the amateur psychiatrist, I think Michael's mother had always been very dominant in his life and thought that his marriage break-down was her perfect chance to move in and be the doting grandmother, helping to look after Michael and the children. The arrival of me on the scene had completely quashed all her plans and so she was trying to drive me away, whether consciously or unconsciously. We thought about having a confrontation with her and then decided it would be in nobody's interest, especially the children's. So we simply played along with her, making sure the children understood the true position at all times, and trying desperately hard to rise above her allegations. Up to a point it has worked – she is certainly less vindictive than she was – but I'll never be able to forgive her for what she's done.

A final word of warning: children are very possessive about relationships. While in the long term it may be a good idea to introduce your children and stepchildren to the joys of everyone's grandparents, be very wary of doing this too early on. In other words, allow the children to keep their grandparents to themselves and only mix them up at their suggestion, as and when the step-family becomes more solid and secure.

Aunts, uncles and cousins

Uncles and aunts can be very important in children's lives, or they can be extremely remote. Like grandparents, a favourite aunt or uncle could provide continuity and a sense of security in a changing world, and if such a relationship exists then special care should be taken to preserve it. Cousins, too, can fulfil this role. Particularly when the children are teenagers and young adults, they may find talking through a family problem with their cousins is the perfect solution – they are contemporaries, so they understand, but they are also family and so the children do not feel disloyal.

As a step-parent, be careful not to foist your brothers, sisters, nephews and nieces on to your new stepchildren with too much enthusiasm. The introduction of a large extended stepfamily can be very overwhelming for children. They have an awful lot to come to terms with, and so new relationships should be taken on board slowly. Why should they be expected to kiss 'Auntie May' and 'Uncle George', whom they have never met before, to whom they are in no way related by blood, and who in any event may well just come to see them out of curiosity. This is important – in the early days, try and expose the children only to those members of the family who really have their best interests at heart. They need to be surrounded by as much positive thinking as possible, and only when they feel secure can the more controversial members of the family be introduced with confidence.

A helpful 'game' you can play is to draw up a family tree. Start with the two separate families and then bring them together, so that the children can see a pictorial image of how the family structure works, which in turn will make it seem a lot less daunting. If you can, get a photograph of every member of the family and paste these beside their names, which will make the family tree look both cheerful and more interesting. New members can be added with great ceremony, and the whole thing could prove a very reassuring and helpful document.

The family is a weird and wonderful institution. Most of the truly ghastly crimes we read about in the press are committed within the family. The worst emotional pain which one human being can inflict upon another is usually found within the framework of a family. Yet despite these facts a large family is reassuring. Maybe there are certain members whom you do not actually like or would at best never choose to spend any time with, but this is not necessarily important. The family rituals surrounding various celebrations, from the birth of a new baby to Granny and Grandpa's Golden Wedding, all serve to build up solidarity in this changing, sometimes confusing world. The fact that Uncle Jack always gets drunk, that Aunt Maud can't stop bitching, that little Jennifer is always sick because she eats too much and that Grandad insists on making one of his long-winded, incomprehensible speeches is all part of the fabric which binds families together and gives them a sense of belonging.

Your focus should clearly rest upon your partner and those children living with you and to whom you have access. None the less, the extended family can have a vital role to play. There will have been other divorces, other stepchildren, other remarriages, perhaps not in this generation but in the previous one. The family unit has seen it all before: it can absorb the dramas and put them in perspective. If you can, do your best to gather the family around you – it may prove to be your best possible asset.

6

The Artificial Family

One of the most difficult tasks ever to beset a parent is the welding together of a family unit which comprises a number of children of unequal status: 'hers', who live with the family, 'his', who visit; and 'theirs', the new baby, whom everyone loves to hate. How do you cope with trying to raise your own natural child on equal terms with a stepchild who may in looks and temperament remind you constantly of the man or woman you replaced in your partner's life?

Some parents handle this situation by over-compensating the child or children they cannot love, and actually depriving their own natural children whom they do love, in a desperate effort to redress the balance of their feelings. Other parents simply cannot cope with the needs of their stepchildren, leaving them in an emotional desert; while a minority take out the frustrations of their own unloving childhood by abusing or ill-treating the children who are not theirs by birth.

The unwanted step-parent

Julie's story makes one's blood run cold but, sadly, it is not unfamiliar:

> When I got together with Bill I knew really he'd never take to my daughter, Suzie. We've always been very close, Suzie and I. Her Dad was no good and we went through a lot together. She was dead against my marrying Bill, but I didn't want to be alone. She was twelve, the years were slipping away, and it seemed like it was my last chance.
>
> They were always fighting, Suzie and Bill – he was always trying to impose his will upon her. But she'd had a tough enough life to be able to stick up for herself, and she wasn't going to take any nonsense.

I'm a nurse, and when we'd been married about eight months I had a period of night duty. You will think this is a crazy thing to say, but when I walked into the house that morning I could tell by the atmosphere what had happened. Normally I used to creep into the kitchen, make a coffee and then stagger up to bed. But that particular morning I just stood in the hall and listened.

At first I could hear nothing but the traffic outside, and then I heard this sound. At first I couldn't make out what it was, but when I climbed the stairs I recognised that it was someone, Suzie, crying, very softly, in a muffled way. I went into her bedroom. She was cowering under the bedclothes – it's the only way I can describe it – completely crumpled. I knew immediately that Bill had abused her – no, why mince my words? – raped her, a twelve-year-old girl.

I asked her directly what had happened. As I said, we'd always had a good relationship, and she told me immediately – not hiding anything, not dramatising either, struggling to get the words out in between the tears.

At that moment I wanted to kill him, but I knew I would only be heaping more agony on Suzie. I told her we were leaving. I got our suitcases out of the cupboard and packed for her while she sat there.

In our bedroom, Bill was lying in a drunken sleep. When I looked at him I could see him as nothing more than an animal, a filthy animal. I packed quickly and quietly, but he was too drunk to hear me. We reported him, not because we wanted vengeance for ourselves but in case he did the same thing to another little girl. He went to prison, and it was no more than he deserved.

Suzie seems to have come through it all very well, but I will never forgive myself for what I inflicted upon her. My selfish need for companionship, someone to love, a man, caused her all this suffering. It must have scarred her.

What I cannot understand is why I went ahead with marrying Bill when I knew that he and Suzie would never work out. Of course I never anticipated what happened, but I did recognise that he would never be a good stepfather to her. Yet I went ahead, against my better instincts, and that's what I've got to live with.

First, let's look at the situation from the child's point of view. Jealousy is one of the most destructive of all feelings and also one of the strongest. Children who are feeling jealous of a new step- or half-sibling in many instances deliberately make themselves as unpleasant as possible, to test the love of their parent. This in turn does not endear them to their new step-parent, and everyone's relationships suffer just at a moment which is probably already high on tension and stress.

Alternatively, they may develop apparently unconnected symptoms of an illness, genuinely physical in content, from which they seem unable to recover. This, of course, is an attention-seeker. While their parent is worried about them they can be sure of staying centre-stage. Another classic symptom concerns school – a sudden drop-off in quality of work, bad behaviour or even truancy may be an attempt to test where the child stands in this new family.

For it is a fact, though not an easy one to swallow, that the joy a lonely couple may feel at finding one another and bringing their families together under one roof is in their children's eyes a cause for nothing but pain. Ask Oliver:

> We didn't need him or want him in our lives. We were doing very well on our own. Our mother had always been such a sensible and nice person, but when he arrived she went all sort of silly. She didn't seem to have a mind of her own any more. Whatever he wanted was what happened. It was ghastly – it still is. Jamie and I are going to leave home as soon as we can, in my case only a couple of years' time. We just can't understand why she did it.

Ask almost any child being brought up by a single parent how they would feel about their parent remarrying, and nearly always the truthful answer is that they would hate it. These children have become used to coping without two full-time parents, and the return to the status quo can only represent a threat.

Let's look at the different types of sibling relationships.

The new baby

It is a very natural thing for a couple who already have children by other partners to want a child together. It is probably not quite such a big decision as it is for a more conventional couple who have not been married before. Existing parents will be well aware of the big upheaval involved. If you are used to planning your life around the demands of your children, one more child – a child which symbolises your union – does not seem a major complication.

And yet, of course, it is. Like your new marriage, your new baby is a threat because it can be perceived as pushing out the existing children. Again, your joy is your children's pain. This may sound negative, but it is best to be realistic. Nevertheless there are a number of positive aspects to a new baby:

* A new baby in the family can provide a very real and tangible link, because he or she is related to everyone. Where both parents already have children, these children have no blood ties to one another; but they do both have blood ties to the baby. The newcomer can prove to be a very useful catalyst, drawing the family together.

* The baby can provide an outlet for individual members of the stepfamily to offer love and affection in a demonstrative way, which they may not have been able to do for some time. This can particularly apply to adolescents, who desperately need to be demonstrative but often find it difficult, even in conventional family groups.

* A possible extension is that stepchildren may find showing affection for the baby an easy way to express their affection for their step-parent. In other words, while they may have wanted for some time to

demonstrate their feelings towards their step-parent, they may have felt it disloyal to their natural parent to do so. The baby gives them a legitimate channel to express their feelings.

* If the step-parent involved has not been a parent before, the new baby will bring a deeper awareness and understanding of the role and responsibilities of being a parent. Suddenly, much of what they may not have understood to date about their partner's feelings will become apparent.

* Producing a child of the new marriage may help to cement it. A new partner, and a wife in particular, may feel that she is the second-class citizen in her husband's life because she is not the mother of his children. Even when she has been married to him longer than the first wife was she may feel a tendency to under-rate herself – a new baby will help her to feel of equal status to the first wife.

Let's now look at the negative aspects:

* Just at a time when the other children may have begun to settle down into the new stepfamily, the arrival of a baby can bring a return of all the old fears that they felt at the time of their parent's break-up and remarriage – rejection, anger and jealousy may rise to the surface again. It may prove to be yet another adjustment which is too painful to handle.

* Children may well be confused by the adverse feelings they experience. The conventions of society will tell them that people are supposed to be pleased when a new baby is expected, and so they will be worried and upset by their own unpleasant thoughts. Somehow they need to be reassured that their feelings are perfectly natural and not at all wrong, even if they do not conform to what is considered normal. Unless this problem is recognised and dealt with, the child will be consumed with guilt – a guilt he or she does not even understand.

* Mothers are very protective of their newborn infants, even when the older siblings are their own. The idea of grubby children handling their new piece of perfection is almost too much to bear. When the older siblings are not theirs, and if their general standard of behaviour is low anyway, the arrival of the new baby may break the tight rein the stepmother has kept on her true feelings. Suddenly, she will be unable to control her anger and frustration at the way her stepchildren behave. This in itself can create a huge crisis. What applies to full-time stepchildren applies equally to visiting stepchildren.

* Stepchildren will very quickly come to realise that the new baby is their parents' Achilles heel, particularly if the natural parent is their father rather than their mother. If their father remarrying has caused the children pain they will never blame him – only the woman he married. This woman is now vulnerable, and by upsetting the baby the children can get even for all the pain that, as they see it, the stepmother has caused them.

  All this, of course, is likely to be subconscious or at least partly so. It is not a planned vendetta, but can result in stepchildren deliberately making a noise to wake a new baby, teasing or upsetting it and, in more extreme cases, committing an act of violence towards the baby.

* As the new baby grows into a child the threat it represents to the other children may diminish as they grow to love it and settle into the new family. But this may not happen, and unavoidable problems may arise. On the face of it, the new child may seem much more privileged than his siblings. He basks in the love and affection of both parents, he has a settled home life, no pressures from warring parents, no adjustments to make because of living in more than one home. As things settle down within the new family it may be that finances improve, so that the child

enjoys a better standard of living than did his siblings during the turbulent years of their parents' split-up.

* Finally, if the older siblings are suffering from any form of behavioural problems the parents, particularly the natural parent of the new child, will be worried about this behaviour affecting the newcomer. This may cause great friction.

All things considered, an addition to the family is bound to create something of an emotional minefield. There is no right time to have a new baby. There are grounds for saying that, while everything is new and disorganised, you might as well go ahead and add to the confusion – to get it all over with. Alternatively, you might take the view that it is better to settle the existing children before embarking on creating another. It depends what you feel is best for you and yours.

If you are feeling daunted by all this, perhaps Irene's uplifting story will cheer you:

> I met Chris when I went as a temporary relief teacher to the school where he is head of the history department. We talked a few times in the staff room and I liked him. He is nine years older than me and I simply assumed he was married. It wasn't until we both became involved in an end-of-term play that I talked to him more and found that he was divorced. We started going out together, and from the first I had no doubts he was the right man for me.
>
> Chris's first marriage ended when his wife, Jane, ran off with someone else whom she subsequently married. Chris and Jane had one son, Oliver, who was six when Chris and I met.
>
> Right from the beginning I could tell that the fact that his son lived with his wife hurt Chris very much indeed. He was clearly very fond of the little boy and felt considerable pain at being separated from him. The divorce had obviously been very acrimonious, and Chris and Jane hardly spoke. Chris was very bitter that Jane had not only left him but had taken their child too.

At the time a lot of this was mere speculation on my part because Chris always found – and, indeed, still does find – difficulty in expressing his feelings. It's strange, really, because he's so good with the children at his school – really impressive, really communicative.

Anyway, Chris and I married and eventually I plucked up the courage to suggest that we considered having a family of our own. To begin with he was very reluctant. I couldn't understand it – his whole work and life were dedicated to children and he loved his son, so why didn't he want any more?

Eventually he told me the reason. He was frightened, very frightened, that he would make another emotional commitment to a child and then lose him, like he had lost Oliver. I swore to him that, no matter what happened to our relationship, I'd never do that to him. But he was still doubtful.

It was about this time that we reached agreement with Jane that we could see Oliver once a month for the day. Initially Oliver was very wary of me, so I made sure that I kept a very low profile when he was around and gradually he seemed to become quite fond of me. He clearly adored his father – it was very touching seeing them together. This contact with Oliver softened Chris's attitude to the idea of another child, and we agreed to try for a baby.

When I became pregnant we waited for some time before we told Oliver. He was very quiet when he heard the news, and it worried us a great deal. When Chris was driving him home to his mother's house, he asked his Dad whether he'd still want to see him when the new baby arrived. It was heartbreaking, awful. Chris did everything he could to reassure him. He was very depressed that night, and I began to wonder whether I'd done the right thing in persuading him that we should have a family of our own.

We tried to involve Oliver in the preparation for the baby as much as we could, which was difficult because, since we only saw him on Sundays, we couldn't take him shopping. Gradually he seemed to get used to the idea, but tended to change the subject if we mentioned it. I began to hope desperately that the child would be a girl, assuming that this would be less direct competition for Oliver to cope with.

Our son, Edward, was born just before Christmas. He was a lovely baby. Chris was with me, and he cried when the baby was born. I was really surprised – he showed his emotions in front of the nurses and everyone.

As soon as we were all home, we arranged with Jane that Oliver should come over for the day. She was unexpectedly co-operative, which we both found strange and a little worrying. I was so nervous waiting for Oliver to arrive – I kept telling Chris to be really careful, not to show too much affection for Edward while Oliver was about, and that I would look after the baby so that he could concentrate on Oliver.

When Oliver arrived he didn't ask to see the baby. So after a rather awkward conversation for about ten minutes, Chris said, 'Come and see Edward.' We all trooped upstairs to Edward's room. He was asleep in his crib. Oliver looked at him for a few moments and said, suddenly, 'He's nice.'

'I'll tell you something,' Chris said. 'He looks exactly like you did when you were born. In fact when he was born, Irene will tell you, I made a bit of a fool of myself and cried, because he looked so like you.'

It was the perfect thing to have said. 'Does he really?' Oliver said. 'Did you really cry? That was soppy, Daddy.'

I was close to tears myself and left them to it. By the end of the day Oliver was helping change Edward's nappy and was really keen on his little brother. Much to our surprise, when he asked his mother if he could come a fortnight later she was again very co-operative, and it was on this next visit that we discovered why. She was up to her old tricks again – her new husband had left the family home and she was seeing someone else.

Edward is two now, and just before his second birthday he had his best present ever – Oliver came to live with us permanently. I may sound bitchy, but I think it was simply that he doesn't fit in with his mother's love life any more. We're such a happy family now and the boys are really close. We've been very lucky.

Lucky they may have been, but thoughtful and considerate as well. Chris and Irene deserve their happiness because Oliver's feelings have always been considered and given priority.

Resident siblings

When two people meet and marry and bring children to their new marriage, it is likely that those children have of late been living in a single-parent family. Being part of a single-parent family, once children are used to it, is not so bad. There are disadvantages, of course. Usually there is not enough money about. The single parent is likely to have to work, so that part of the younger child's day will be spent with a childminder or nanny or in a crèche. But once the parent and child are reunited at the end of the day within the home, the child has one hundred per cent of the parent's attention. There is no other adult relationship to get in the way.

Understandably, many single parents fall into the trap of spoiling their children – allowing them to sleep in their bed, to stay up late and take part in adult social activities. They do so as much for their own sake as for the child's, because they are lonely. Then suddenly they are not lonely any more; they have found someone with whom they want to spend the rest of their lives. Inevitably the children are relegated to their traditional role and cease to be considered as companions. It is never an easy situation, but when this is complicated by both partners bringing children to the marriage it can be a disaster.

If your collective children are all roughly the same age, on the face of it you would think that this makes things easier; in fact it does not. Long ago the social services identified that, when children are adopted, it is far better for there to be a natural gynaecological gap between each child rather than to crowd them too closely together in age. Where two or three children, all much of an age, are suddenly thrust together into a family, competition will be rife. They will all be expecting the same things from their parents. They will all want to play with each other's toys, because they are appropriate to all of them. Bedtime will be the same, so there is no chance to talk individually to the children at special times of the day – and so on, and so on.

In this situation the worst thing you can do is make any sort of assumption that the children will be friends, or even like each other. Just because you love his Dad, there is no reason why he should love your daughter, or vice versa. Having said that, Liz's story makes lovely reading:

I met Graham when he'd been widowed for six months. He had a three-year-old daughter, Jennifer. I also had a daughter, Gill, who was just four months older than Jennifer. My husband had deserted us soon after Gill was born.

Both Graham and I were free to marry, both lonely, and so our relationship developed very quickly. What we were not sure about was the girls. They'd shown a guarded interest in each other when we'd introduced them, but friends were very quick to point out that two children so close in age would never get along together – they would always compete.

We decided to ignore our 'good advice', but at the same time recognised the very real problems the girls were likely to experience. I gave up work, and for the first six months employed a very nice woman from the village to come and help me with the children. It was not so much that I needed help with the domestic chores, but more that I needed someone else around to reduce the element of competition for my time. In other words, each girl had somebody to give her exclusive time and attention.

We tried to keep this up for most of the first year together, avoiding as many situations as possible which could lead to putting them into a position of conflict. For example, Graham came home from work in time to help me put them to bed, so that I didn't have to make decisions as to who I kissed good-night first or whose bed we had the story in.

It may seem as though we over-reacted to the problems as we saw them. So I was enormously reassured when a social worker, in conversation at a party, was very quick to outline the recurrent problems which can emerge from trying to raise two children, within the same family, who are closer in age than a normal biological gap would allow.

Certainly what we have today is two little girls who are very good friends, who really don't seem to need anyone else. They play together for hours and miss each other dreadfully if they are parted. In fact I would go so far as to say that they are probably better friends than normal sisters would be. Obviously the main reason is that they are two genuinely nice children, who have not been outrageously jealous and are by nature friendly.

Having said that, I do think the time and trouble we took to establish their relationship was well worthwhile. When Jennifer starts full-time school next September I will probably go back to work part-time, but I don't regret for a moment these valuable two years, when my main priority has been to turn us into a family.

On the plus side, small children can be reassured by suddenly having two people to look after them; and, surprisingly perhaps, teenagers can be quite sympathetic to the concept of their parent having a new relationship. Indeed, teenagers may find their parent's budding love life something of a relief after the perhaps rather claustrophobic hot-house atmosphere of their one-to-one relationship with their single parent. Here, therefore, is a situation which can be a recipe for success, so long as you recognise that the teenager is unlikely to want to be part of the stepfamily as such. In other words, if Mum's found a new fella and he's making her happy, fine; but the teenager's going to take a pretty dim view of Mum's new man expecting to be called Dad and starting to lay down the law as to what time the teenager should be home. This equally applies to step-siblings – the older child or teenager might be quite prepared to welcome a new partner in their parent's life, even if that new partner includes a younger child or children, provided that the children are not thrust on him as his new 'brother or sister'.

So whatever the mix of children and whatever their

ages, their relationship must be allowed to evolve naturally and not be forced in any way. As far as you, the parents, are concerned your expectations should be nil. Here is a horror story which happened to one particular family, told by their teenage daughter Sophie. It makes sombre reading:

Ann and I had been best friends at school since we were twelve. Our families became quite friendly as a result. Ann has two brothers, one older and one younger, and I have a younger brother and an older sister, so we all fitted together quite well. We used to get together at weekends for picnics and things, and once we had a holiday in Italy in a self-catering villa, which was great.

Ann and I didn't suspect anything for ages, though I think my older sister, Daisy, had her suspicions. The first time I realised anything was wrong was when I came home from school early and found Mum crying in the kitchen. She didn't tell me what was wrong, except that she'd had a really bad row with Dad. From that moment on the atmosphere in the house deteriorated, but nobody would tell me what was going on. In the end I forced Daisy into explaining.

My Mum, would you believe, had fallen in love with Ann's father! I just couldn't bear it – there was no way it made any sense. When Daisy told me I went off for a walk on my own and ended up at Ann's house. She didn't know anything about it, so I told her and she refused to believe me. She screamed and yelled at me and told me to go away. At school the next day we didn't speak. Everybody kept asking us what was wrong – it was awful.

It was about a week later that Mum and Dad got us together – Daisy, me and our little brother, Jonathan – and told us that Dad was leaving the house, that they were getting a divorce and it was likely that Mum and Ann's Dad would be getting together at some stage.

I felt really sorry for Dad. He tried to be jolly, and said it would be nice for me because Ann would be my sister. I didn't want Ann to be my sister – I had a sister. Ann was just my friend. Mum kept on saying she was sorry over and over again.

If she was so sorry, why did she let it happen?

Dad left and moved into a flat about half a mile away, and about three months later it was decided that we should move into Ann's house. Her mother had gone off, too, to live with her parents somewhere in Dorset. It was ghastly. Of course they put me in a room with Ann because we were such good friends, but the truth was that Ann and I weren't friends at all any more – we positively hated each other. Daisy refused to come, and left home. And I felt really sorry for Jonathan because he didn't like either of Ann's brothers and was really bullied by the older one, George.

The whole thing is horrible, horrible, and I don't believe Mum's even happy. She is very thin and looks tired all the time and I often know she's been crying. It would never have happened if Ann and I hadn't been best friends.

This is a true story of what can happen to two nice families in a moment of madness, and from the sound of Sophie's story nobody is happy with the result. Perhaps the saddest thing of all, since parents are responsible for their own actions, is the breakdown of Sophie and Ann's friendship just at a time when they each desperately needed a good friend. It's easy to see why – Sophie's last sentence makes it clear. Both girls feel terribly guilty about what's happened and they can't bear to continue with something which has created so much pain for everyone.

One of the added problems in this particular family is the fact that all the children are very close in age. You might think that since they have all spent so much time together it would be easy to become one big happy family. But it won't happen when there are two parents missing – two parents left high and dry without a family or a home.

Home and away siblings

This is a very common occurrence – the children of the wife tend to live in the new home permanently, while the children of the husband are only visitors. As explained already, this problem of unequal status among the children is very difficult. The visitors will always feel like visitors, and the resident children will tend to resent them. There are no easy answers, other than a great deal of tact and patience.

All over the country on Friday nights and Saturday mornings tired parents and reluctant children try to find some common ground, some formula for making the weekend ahead enjoyable. All over the country on Sunday mornings fathers go to collect their children and then try desperately to create some kind of family atmosphere in the few hours allocated to them. There are a few golden rules which apply to home and away siblings:

* Cut down the resentment by trying to disrupt the home siblings' life as little as possible. This could be achieved by making their access weekend the same, so that in fact the two sets of children rarely meet. This may be not such a bad thing initially. Make sure that the visiting children have the right equipment and clothes for the weekend planned. Where a divorce has been particularly vindictive the children may deliberately be sent with the wrong clothes. In this situation you need to build up a stock of items such as wellington boots and swimming costumes, even if they are only hand-me-downs, so that the children are equipped to fit in with your plans. If not, they will feel like outsiders.

* Try and give the visiting children a regular routine while they are with you. They should not be simply allowed to come in and behave as they like or refuse to help. To give them security and make them feel it's their home too you will also need to apply discipline where appropriate, though slowly and gently at first.

* On the visiting weekends don't become involved in visits to grandparents or aunts, where only part of the family is truly welcome and every opportunity is made to highlight the 'separateness' of the two sets of

children. On visiting weekends you are a family – you are all to be treated as such, or not at all.

* With older children, make sure that they really do want to come to stay in the form that may have been agreed on their behalf some years before. Most teenagers' idea of a weekend is to spend at least fifty per cent of the day in bed, Friday and Saturday night out with their friends, and Sunday night in a mad, grumpy rush to finish their homework for Monday morning. None of this is very compatible with an access weekend to the non-custodial parent, and so as the child gets older it might be possible for the visits to take place for a slightly longer period during the school holidays.

These two types of sibling relationship breed resentment very easily, not only among children but also among parents, for the visiting children often disrupt and unsettle the normal family unit. Just remember, always, that the children did not create this situation – they had it thrust upon them. It is not their fault that they are thrust from pillar to post. Try to understand, and be kind.

Visiting siblings

In theory it is far easier for a couple not coping with children on a day-to-day basis to accept visits from siblings normally resident somewhere else. In practice, however, this is not always the case. For a couple who are not geared up to children, and who in most instances will have one partner who has not had any previous experience of parenthood, the drama of these visits can loom very large indeed.

Disruption is the key word here. The partner whose children they are will suddenly become to his other half a more remote figure. He (for they are usually Dads in this situation) will become a parent first, a marriage partner second. The house will degenerate into a tip, things will get broken, huge meals will need to be cooked, invitations have to be turned down, routines are lost. If you are not particularly enamoured at the concept of parenthood, then stepchildren coming to visit can be a pain.

Perhaps you work very hard during the week and you feel your weekends are sacred. You want to spend them relaxing with your husband, catching up on some sleep and going out to dinner. Instead, a horde of children who are not yours, who uncomfortably remind you of your husband's former wife, descend on you and you spend the whole weekend as a drudge. How can you explain your fury and resentment to your husband? You love him, he loves them and that should be enough – but, of course, it isn't.

Try to understand that the non-custodial parent is in a difficult situation. A father will tend to be resentful about the fact that he is probably paying maintenance for his children while the bulk of their time is spent with their mother and perhaps stepfather – a stepfather who will be gaining a close relationship with his children, which he will never achieve again. A mother will feel guilty – she will feel judged by society if the children to whom she gave birth do not live with her. There are all sorts of guilts and jealousies at work here, and if you are to be happy in your marriage you must accept that this is as much a part of your partner as the nose on his face.

As ever, try and put yourself in the position of the child: 'It's bad enough not having Mummy and Daddy living together any more. Now Daddy has got a new wife and she doesn't even seem to like us. We miss Daddy, and yet when we see him we feel uncomfortable.' It's not fair, is it, put like that? Childhood is so brief and, however unacceptable or difficult your partner's visiting children may be today, in a year's time they will be quite different and five years from now entirely different. Their childhood is very precious and already disrupted. Try and make things as good for them as you possibly can.

Presenting a face to the world

When a new stepfamily get together, one of the things that each member tries to do is to appear normal to the outside world. It is a well-established fact that children have to be different, but so indeed do adults. Everyone wants to appear to be a happy part of a happy family. Appearing to be a normal family is fine, provided that you do not lose sight of your family's origins. Always be prepared to talk about the past with the children, about changing relationships and – however difficult – about their parent's marriage.

The social services help fostered and adopted children to create a cover story to help them with enquiries from casual acquaintances and school friends. This means they do not need to explain all the complications of their background unless they wish to. These cover stories are not lies as such, but are usually based on the truth. In response to an enquiry, for example, as to why Tom is living with a lady down the road, his answer could be that his mother works nights. His mother may well have worked nights at some point in her life. The fact that the family home has broken down and she can no longer cope with her children is not something that Tom wants to discuss in detail. It is too painful for him, and he doesn't consider it necessarily his school friends' business. So he becomes adapt at fending off enquiries which he feels are too intimate. It is good protection, particularly in the early days following a trauma, and you could develop cover stories for your children if they feel they need them.

In a completely different way we have a problem such as this within our own family:

> Our natural son, Charlie, is six months younger than his adopted brother, Michael. Extraordinarily, the boys look very alike, are very similar in height and are naturally assumed to be twins. We are endlessly asked questions about them and at first we were floundering as to how to reply. Now we have a formula.

In response to the question, 'Are they twins?' we say, 'No, they are brothers.'

That never satisfies the enquirier. He or she then says, 'They must be very close in age. What's the age difference?'

We reply, 'Six and a half months – one is ours by adoption and the other is ours by birth.' We never say which is which! I am sure that in the years ahead the boys will have quite a lot of fun getting people to guess their identity, for it is certainly not obvious.

In this instance, of course, it is not a cover story but simply a way of dealing with questions. It is extraordinary how the most casual acquaintance seems to feel it is their right to know every detail of your family. Years ago, within our own family, we decided to banish the words 'step' and 'half'; everybody is a brother or a sister. It works very well, and it also saves on explanations.

Despite all the grim and dire warnings in this chapter, the artificial family can be quite as loving and secure as any so-called 'normal' family. It takes time, patience, tact and humour, but in the long term, the results can be deeply satisfying.

7

What's In A Name?

For very understandable reasons, on the formation of a new stepfamily the parents often feel a strong desire to tidy things up, to make them seem to all the world like a 'normal' family. One aspect which stands out like a sore thumb is children with different surnames from their parents. This, of course, occurs when a mother remarries. Children hate being different, so is it not sensible to change their name to that of their stepfather's, particularly if they are not really in touch with their natural father? After all, it avoids all those complications at school and with new friends who did not even know the former family. My own former married name was Mackillop, and I have lost count of the times that my husband has been referred to as Mr Mackillop as opposed to Mr Fowler. Luckily he takes a philosophical attitude, seeing it as part of the job of being a stepfather. I can understand, though, that not all men would feel like this – yet is a stepfather's momentary irritation so important?

To change or not to change

The social services and other professional bodies generally consider it undesirable to change children's names, even if their father has little or no contact with them. However ineffective the father, one can see the logic of this argument. Perhaps, too, it is more important for children whose fathers have neglected or ignored them to maintain his name. After all, his name may be the only really tangible thing he has ever given them. Douglas is clearly not conventional father material, yet it is interesting how strongly he feels about this issue.

I lost touch with my children when they were still babies. My wife and I split up in very bitter circumstances. I'm not saying it was her fault, it was mine – I simply fell in love with someone else. I tried to go on seeing the children, but it was difficult. My wife lives in Cumbria and my new girlfriend and I lived down south. There was never time at the weekends somehow to make the trip north – in any case, my wife made it quite clear that she didn't want me having any contact with the kids.

Two years ago my wife remarried. I've met her new husband and he's a nice chap and very good to the children, there's no doubt about it. About six months ago they asked how I would feel about having the children's names changed, so that they all had the same surname. I resisted it strongly, and much to my surprise Phil, my ex-wife's new husband, seemed to understand and talked her out of it.

It's a difficult thing to explain – I know I've been a rotten father to the children, but none the less they are my kids biologically, and maybe one day, when they're older, perhaps even grown up, we'll be friends. The fact that they have my name is the link I have with them.

This man may seem selfish, but his view is backed by statistics. Of those children who have their names changed to that of their stepfather in early life, over fifty per cent change them back to their original name as young adults. It is very difficult to try and make a judgement on how your child will feel when he or she is grown up. Nearly all children will at some stage try and form a link with the missing parent, and a shared name is a starting point. What you have to weigh up is the advantage of a few years' convenience as opposed to the possible resentment your child may feel as a young adult if in his or her eyes you have taken the law into your own hands. The inconvenience really is minimal. When I have to telephone Lucy's school, for example, because she is ill, I simply say, 'This is Lucy Mackillop's Mum speaking,' rather than run the risk of the secretary being confused by me saying, 'It's Mrs Fowler. Would you tell Lucy's form teacher she will be off school today?' Not exactly onerous, is it?

If an older child – particularly after having lived with a stepfather for some years – suddenly announces that he or she would like to take the stepfather's name, then of course this is a completely different matter. Such a request can and should be viewed as a tremendous compliment to the stepfather. Clearly he has earned his spurs and deserves to be called Dad, and the child wants some tangible token belonging to him.

Such a request should be recognised for what it is – a huge commitment on the child's behalf. It must be taken very seriously by the parents and acted upon as soon as possible. To treat it as something casual and unimportant – 'We're a family anyway, aren't we?' – will be perceived by the child as rejection. Let's face it, it's not dissimilar to getting married. How would you feel if your partner greeted your marriage proposal with casualness and no sense of occasion?

Carrying on the family name

Ten-year-old Roger has an interesting story to tell. He lives in Oxford with his mother, sister and stepfather, and they are very happy family. Roger's parents split up when he was only a year old. He cannot remember living with his natural father, and when he was three his mother and stepfather changed his and his sister's surname.

> I don't know my Dad – my real Dad, that is – very well. He's a doctor and he travels all over the world selling medicine, so he's not very often at home. However this year – for the first time ever, I think – he was in Oxford on my birthday and took me out to lunch. We had a good talk about all sorts of things. I don't think he thought I was old enough to bother with before, and he always says he's not very good with children.
>
> Just before we finished lunch, he asked me how I felt about having had my name changed. I'd never thought about it

before. I had just thought my name had always been the same as my stepfather's, and I hadn't realised that Mum had changed it. It made me feel funny – cross, I think. Dad said he hoped that one day I might change it back to his. He said he hadn't argued about it at the time because he didn't want a row, but I'm the only boy of my generation in the family and the name will die out unless I change it back.

I thought about it a lot afterwards. I thought about talking to Mum and Dad about it – my step-Dad, that is – but decided not to and talked to my elder sister, Julia, instead. She said I was making a fuss about nothing. It doesn't matter in her case, because one day she'll get married and change her name anyway. But that won't happen to me, and I can't help feeling that my real Dad is right – when I'm old enough I think I will change my name back to his.

Maybe Roger's father was a bit naughty to raise this issue and worry his son. On the other hand maybe he was right to do so because, clearly, unless he had raised the matter, it would not have occurred to Roger that his name had been changed at all – at any rate for some years. It is worrying that he doesn't feel he can talk to his mother and stepfather, even though he is cross with them. I'd like to bet he will change his name when he is older.

Arguably, it could be said that it is more important for boys' names to be left unchanged than it is for girls. Certainly this is the point Roger's father is making. However, with the establishment of sex equality this does not seem right. Boy or girl, everyone is born an individual and has a right to an individual name, whether they keep it for life or until marriage. Clearly if the child is pressing to have his or her name changed, you should do your best to achieve this for them. If, however, the idea is really your own and the child is either too young to have any definite views or has expressed no preference, it is better to leave well alone.

Adoption: for and against

A more drastic way of regularising the position of a stepfamily is to apply for a step-parent adoption. A number of issues should be taken into account before you even consider such a move.

* Courts on the whole are reluctant to grant a step-parent adoption, unless there is absolutely no other way of achieving stability for the child.

* As a married couple, the natural parent and step-parent both have to adopt the child. This seems rather an odd way of going about things, but it is how the law operates.

* Couples who are not married cannot adopt children as a couple. This does not preclude single individuals from adopting a child; but a couple living together, however long they may have cohabited, are not eligible.

* The social services are always involved. They have to produce what is known as a Schedule 2 Report for the court, concerning the suitability of parent and step-parent, and a report on the situation with regard to the other natural parent.

* The consent of the other natural parent is required, although in very special circumstances the judge can waive this requirement.

* The children concerned will be interviewed by the social services if they are seven or older, so it is extremely important that they understand what is happening.

* In theory a couple can apply to adopt a child as little as three months after marriage. In practice, however, the social services are unlikely to support a step-parent adoption unless the couple have been married for at least a year.

The court's reluctance to support a step-parent adoption is based on the belief that there is usually a better way of achieving the same end. Let's consider for a moment why you and your partner might wish to adopt the natural children of one of you.

The best motive, and indeed the only one which cuts much ice with the courts, is a genuine need to protect the child. If the child's absent parent is an abuser or a rapist, or has a history of violence towards the child, this would certainly be grounds for adoption. If the missing parent is in prison, receiving long-term psychiatric care or has simply disappeared off the face of the earth, having played little or no part in the child's life, here again there are grounds for an adoption. Above all, of course, if the other parent is dead it is very understandable that the parent and step-parent may feel that adoption will really cement their family and give the child, even if there is a supportive extended family.

The nightmare for most single natural parents is the thought that, if they should die, they would be leaving their child's future uncertain or at risk. A step-parent can be awarded a Residence Order by the court, but this is not a final binding arrangement. It can be varied and it can be appealed against. Adoption, by contrast, is for ever. Adoption means that no one can take the children way, provided they are loved and cared for. Brian's story proves the point:

> My wife, Rosemary, died of a rare blood disorder when she was thirty-six. I was left with two small children, both girls – our daughter, Toni, who was two, and Pauline, aged eight, who is my step-daughter, Rosemary's child by her former marriage. Pauline doesn't know her father at all – Bill left the family home very soon after she was born. Rosemary and I met when Pauline was still a baby and as far as she's concerned I'm her Dad, although, of course, we've always explained to her that I'm not her natural father.
>
> When your wife is only thirty-six, you never assume anything is going to happen to her. I suppose, looking back on it,

we should have taken some precautions to secure the children's future in case one or both of us died, but you can't go through life looking for disasters.

In the weeks immediately following Rosemary's death I was too involved with the children to think about anything much – comforting them and reorganising our lives so we could cope. I am an illustrator and arranged with the agency that employs me that I should work two days a week at home. We already had a part-time mother's help and she agreed to work full-time. So although their mother's death was terrible for the children, their day-to-day lives were not too disrupted.

The letter was a complete bombshell. Pauline's father and girlfriend wanted her. If I wouldn't hand her over, they were going to take me to court. It was the worst nightmare of my life – in a way, almost more terrible than Rosemary dying. I knew how dreadfully I would be letting Rosemary down if I allowed her daughter to go to a man who I knew was a drunkard who had no job or permanent home and whom Pauline did not even know.

Pauline and Toni had always got on well from the moment Toni was born, but with their mother's death the two little girls had become even closer. The three of us were suffering, but we were a team and we were together and, I thought, safe. Now, suddenly, nothing was safe.

It was nearly two years before we were able to feel secure. I cannot tell you what we went through – with court proceedings and welfare officers. It is unusual for a step-parent rather than a natural parent to be given custody, and my lawyer had to work very hard indeed to prove that Pauline should stay with me. Of course at her age I couldn't keep the problem from her – she had to be involved, and her view was needed. It brought terrible pressure upon her, just at the time when she should have been left alone to come to terms with her mother's death. One minute she'd been a happy sunny little girl, living in a secure family. The next, her whole world was in tatters.

I still don't know whether we would have won the case but for the fact that one day, absolutely at my wits' end, I went to see Bill's girlfriend and begged her to exert some influence on Bill. I explained what Pauline had been through and told her about the child's nightmares and panic attacks, which were in no way connected with her mother's death – just the thought of being taken away from me and Toni. I told her everything, and in the end she was in tears and agreed to help.

I presume she did, for eventually Bill withdrew his application – it was either his girlfriend's influence or the fact he had begun to be tired of the whole thing. There was no question of him wanting Pauline for herself. I think it was just a whim. He thought, on hearing that Rosemary had died, that he'd give parenthood a try.

Life is back on an even keel now. Pauline has started at secondary school and Toni is now at school, too, so I am coping far better. The girls are happy and secure but I have no doubt at all that the terrible period during which Pauline thought she might have to leave us has left a scar which will never heal, not completely.

In many situations natural parents' terror of what might become of their children in the event of their death could drive them into seeking adoption. But the child's point of view should be the primary consideration.

So far as older children are concerned, adoption is confusing. They will know that their stepfather is not their real father. What might have been a happy relationship, before adoption is raised as an issue, may turn into resentment if such a step is not what the child really wants. If, for whatever reason, you truly believe that adoption is the right answer for your children, assuming the children are old enough, it is really very important that their views are understood and respected.

It is best if the natural parent seeking to adopt talks first to the child on his or her own, so that the child has the opportunity of expressing a genuine view without being afraid of hurting the step-parent. But do ask yourselves the question which inevitably the court will ask you, 'Why is such a step necessary?' For while it may safeguard the child's future, it takes away the child's rights. The absent natural parent will no longer have any rights to the child and the child can expect nothing from them – their relationship is at an end. Are you and your partner really justified in taking such a drastic step?

How to go about a step-parent adoption

Your starting-point should be the social services department of your local authority. You can apply initially direct to the court, but the court will do nothing until they have a social services report. You will be granted a preliminary meeting with an appointed social worker and, if she feels that your reasons are valid, she will agree to go ahead and produce a Schedule 2 Report which will include every detail about you. They will need to know about your financial position, to see police repots, to know your views on a vast variety of family matters; they will need to see your home and the number of bedrooms it has – it is a fairly lengthy process.

They will also need to seek the permission of the other natural parent, if possible. If the parent is missing, they will do the best they can to find him (it is more often than not the father). If he refuses to give permission the circumstances have to be exceptional for the court to progress in the teeth of such opposition. If the parent realistically cannot be traced this will not jeopardise the adoption in any way – in fact it will tend to prove that there are grounds for it.

In theory, the father of an illegitimate child has no rights. In other words, he cannot block adoption by a mother and stepfather. In practice, though, this may be possible if the father can demonstrate that he has played an active and ongoing part in the child's life. If, however, he has had little or no contact then his agreement is not required.

As already mentioned, children of seven or over will also need to be interviewed. Apparently this is something which a great many parents baulk at. This in itself is worrying, because it suggests that they have not explained the situation properly to their children. If you are undertaking adoption for the right reasons, and if you have a good relationship with your children, this interview should not be a problem. It certainly will not be a heavy interrogation – just a few gentle questions to ensure that the child really knows what is going on.

For obvious reasons the teller of this story wishes to remain anonymous:

I married Greg three years ago and brought a seven-year-old son with me to the marriage. Greg adores my son and he loves his new stepdad. My son is illegitimate and I do not know the identity of his father. So far I have simply told him that I met his father at a party and I never knew his name – it makes me sound like a slut, but the truth is too painful.

The truth is that I was raped, just a few hundred yards from my parent's home, one Saturday night, about 8.30 in the evening. I never saw my attacker's face – he was wearing a balaclava. To say he was not a violent man is stupid, for rape is a violent attack, but he did not hurt me unduly and, although he did threaten me with a knife, afterwards he was sorry and cried. He said he could not help himself.

When I learned some weeks later that I was pregnant, everyone assumed that I would have an abortion. But I'd always been against abortion – about ending a life – and I'd always wanted children. If my attacker had been without remorse, if he'd been more brutal, then I suppose I might have felt different. However, the fact that he cried made me feel that maybe he was not such a bad man. The police never caught him.

Greg and I decided to go ahead with adopting my son, if only so that it would give him a father, a legal father, but also we feel it will hopefully fudge his interest in the past. I never want him to know how he was conceived, and yet one day I suppose I will have to face some very awkward questions from him. It's not a brilliant solution, but it does seem to be a step in the right direction for us.

The whole adoption process can take up to six months, particularly if there is a delay in tracing a missing parent. In a straightforward case, where perhaps one of the parents is dead and the remaining parent has a well-established, happy marriage, the whole process could be achieved in three months. It will never be less, simply because of the way the courts work.

At some stage you will need to decide whether you wish to appoint a solicitor. In theory there is absolutely no reason why you should, and clearly it will save money not to do so. However, if there are likely to be any contentious issues it is very sensible to appoint a solicitor, preferably one who has experience of adoption, since it is a complex business.

Where adoption varies from most other court hearings is that there is no appeal. If, for any reason, the application to adopt is turned down, that is the end of it – it can never be reopened as an issue. For this reason you and/or your solicitor will attend a number of directions hearings – preliminary discussions with the judge before he makes a judgement. This ensures that all the necessary evidence is assembled, so that the final hearing should be very brief. The child will be issued with a new birth certificate, and the whole procedure will be at an end.

Nicky's story is not a happy one, but it demonstrates how careful you have to be when adopting a child:

It was my aunt who told me. We were at a cousin's wedding, and to be honest we'd all had too much to drink. I was twenty and training to be a nurse at the time. We were talking about marriage generally, and how meeting the right man at the right time was just a question of luck. 'Look at your mother,' my aunt said. 'She was such a pretty girl, yet she falls for the wrong sort of man and ends up pregnant – she was such a straitlaced little thing, too.'

As the words came out, I could see her suddenly realising that she had said something wrong. But, having started, she couldn't stop – I wouldn't let her. The next five minutes changed my life.

I learned that I was the result of an affair my mother had

had with a married man, who in discovering that she was pregnant dumped her. She had met the man whom I'd always assumed to be my father when I was just a few months old. They had married and had two more children, whom I had always assumed were my full brother and sister.

I cannot begin to describe to you what a shock it was – it was such a bolt out of the blue. It had frankly never occurred to me that such a situation could have existed and I was so angry – angry with my mother and father for deceiving me, and angry with my aunt for messing up my tranquil, secure life.

It was nearly a week before I could steel myself to talk to my mother about it. At first I thought she was going to deny it – I suppose I almost hoped she would – and say my aunt had made a terrible mistake. But she didn't. She told me it was true that my father, or rather my stepfather, had adopted me as soon as he and my mother had got together. They thought it best that I should never know, as my natural father was not a pleasant sort of person and had strongly recommended to my mother that she had an abortion.

My reaction to the news surprised me as much as my mother, I think. I had to find my natural father. It was not that I felt any sense of personal rejection, as is the case with some adopted children. I knew he had never known me and I could understand why he had not married my mother, since he was married already. It was not just curiosity, either. Suddenly I didn't know who I was any more, and I had to find him in order to find my own sense of identity again.

It took eight months, and when I did finally track him down it was to learn that he had died five months before – I had just missed him. The loss I felt was enormous – ludicrous, really, for a man I had never met. And, to be honest, I still feel I am searching for something – myself, I suppose. I'm thirty-four now and I've had two broken marriages. I can't seem to settle to anything. I'm constantly restless. I'm not sure I'll ever come to terms with my origins. If only my parents had told me from the beginning.

Nicky's story illustrates the appalling problems that can beset a child who suddenly stumbles across the truth of her origins. Of course today illegitimacy has nothing like the stigma attached to it that it once did, and so there is less need for the circumstances of a child's birth to be kept a secret. None the less, a surprising number of parents do attempt to muddy the trail and consequently deny their child the opportunity of ever making contact with his or her other natural parent.

Of course it is vital that you do everything you can to protect your child or stepchild. At the same time it is important to recognise that childhood is a very small proportion of a person's overall lifespan, and, while a natural parent may prove to be a totally unsatisfactory parent to a small child, he or she might prove to be a good friend to the adult. It is a question again of looking very hard at the child's rights. Are you right to separate the child from his origins? I say all this against a backdrop of being an adoptive parent myself.

Our son was born in Romania, and would have spent his life in orphanage care had he not been adopted. Nevertheless we have gone to enormous lengths to protect and maintain his links with his birth family, believing that at some stage in his life it is likely that we, much as we love him, will not be enough, that he will need to make a journey of self-discovery in order to settle down to his chosen course through life. We do not find this insulting, and it does not undermine our feeling of confidence in our relationship with our son. But he is who he is, and we must respect that. If you respect your child's rights and formulate your decision on that basis, you can be sure you will be making the right one.

8

The Family Wreckers

*Tension, Stress, Resentment
and Bitterness*

'I can't bear even being in the same room as her.'
'The more I do for him, the more he seems to resent it.'
'Just because he wants to sleep with her, it doesn't mean that
I have to call her Mother.'
'They're at each other's throats night and day – I just don't
know where we go from here.'
'No one seems to realise that I have needs, too.'

Cries for help

The trouble is that we all expect too much, both of ourselves and of other people, of relationships, of marriage,
of sex, of just about every human condition. Brain-
washed by television and the media in general, all too
often we feel that the rest of the world can overcome
their problems and meet and beat whatever challenges
are put in their path.

In reality, of course, most of us feel the same sense of
inadequacy but the added difficulty for stepfamilies is
that their problems seem 'different' from conventional
families, and there is little professional help available.
Faced with seemingly impossible difficulties most have
tried to soldier on, papering over the cracks, pretending
that nothing is wrong and that really they are an idyllic
family. This pretence in turn creates its own level of
stress and finally something will snap, with disastrous
consequences.

Things are improving – organisations are being set up
to help both step-parents and stepchildren, and a list of

these can be found on page 138. None the less, these self-help organisations have mostly been the brainchild of individuals who have suffered similar problems. There is no central government-sponsored help-line. If your stepchildren are driving you to distraction, if your marriage is under stress and if you do not know where to turn, there is little point in going to the local social services – they will only be able to help you if you have gone too far and abused your stepchildren or neglected them. In other words, they can only help when it is too late. This is not a dig at the social services, which are staffed by extremely overworked people trying to deal with society's problems. It is just a fact, that, as far as the suffering of stepfamilies are concerned, the priorities are not very high.

I was desperate – there was literally no one to turn to. My husband just didn't know what I was talking about: he couldn't understand why his children were driving me to distraction. My friends got bored with me moaning about them, but I just couldn't cope. I went to my doctor and he prescribed tranquillisers – it was the last thing I needed. What I needed was practical help.

In the end I simply ran away, went back to Dorset where I'd spent my childhood and booked into a guest house under a false name. There was a big fuss in the press and the police were called in. The woman who ran the guest house recognised me from the photograph in the newspapers, and my husband and a policeman arrived to collect me. It was a pretty pathetic attempt to disappear. The next day in the newsaper I noticed that one of the journalists said that my disappearance was simply a cry for help, and of course he was right. But nobody was prepared to listen.

My husband and I parted a few months later, and I felt a complete failure. I still believe, though, I could have made a success of it if I'd had some guidance. I'd never been a parent before and didn't know where to start.

If you and your partner are failing to cope, then guilt drives you in on yourself and makes it difficult to confide in anyone. There is also an underlying sense of panic that if you admit your problems to anybody the children will be taken from you, after what may have been a hard fight to get them in the first place. Suffering stepfamilies live in fear – fear of failure, fear of rejection, fear of being misunderstood – they are literally frightened to communicate.

It's the little things

Surprisingly, perhaps, it is the little things which tend to cause the biggest problems. Horrendous dramas of illness, death or financial ruin sometimes bring a family closer together. It is the small irritants which niggle away, until they become obsessive and create havoc within the family.

> There is a muddy lane which leads to the back of our house – it is a short cut from school. Every day he comes in off the lane and walks straight into the house in his muddy shoes – across the kitchen floor, through the hall and into the lounge, a trail of mud. I've asked him and asked him to take his shoes off. I've left spare shoes by the back door, I've asked his father to speak to him – but it makes no difference. He does it on purpose just to spite me, just to prove I have no rights where he is concerned – I'm not his real mother.

> My new stepfather sniffs all the time. He won't use a handkerchief, just sniffs – it's disgusting. I wouldn't mind so much if he didn't keep telling us how to behave – he says we have bad table manners and tells not to swear. At least I know when to use a handkerchief. I think he's horrible.

> I like to do the washing during the week, so that the weekends are free for George and me to spend with the children. I don't expect the children, even Jane, (although she is sixteen) to do any of the washing and ironing themselves. I'm happy to do it for them, but I do ask that they put their clothes in the bin, every day.
> Jane hoards hers, quite deliberately, then puts everything in

the bin on Friday and moans that she's got nothing to wear when she goes out with her friends at the weekend. It makes me look inefficient. I'm sure George feels I'm discriminating against Jane, purposely not washing her clothes, when in fact she creates more washing than the other three children put together. It's her way of getting back at me.

It's clever, really – there are no cross words between us, she always does as she is asked, it's just this washing thing. She knows and I know what it's all about but it's hopeless expecting anybody to believe me – they think I'm just being hyper-sensitive.

Muddy shoes, sniffing, dirty washing – not the stuff that you would think real-life dramas are made of, and yet you can see how they niggle and corrode a relationship. When you are living cheek by jowl with someone day in, day out, you do not have to do anything very melodramatic to cause them grief.

Children know this better than anyone. We accept the foibles of our own children, and children accept the foibles of their parents, because they have grown up with them. Their odd behaviour patterns and irritating little mannerisms are just a part of them. But when you come into a relationship halfway through, with established living patterns which are not your own, minor incidents have a nasty habit of becoming major ones.

Interestingly, from time to time the social services hold seminars for foster-parents – that wonderful band of dedicated people who offer their homes to traumatised and damaged children, saving them from institutional life. Foster-parents, of course, realise that in most instances their relationship with the children in their care is a temporary one; none the less they want it to be as harmonious as possible. They are not saints – just good, caring people who love children and, like everyone, sometimes fail to cope.

Again and again at these seminars, apparently, they say apologetically that it is the accumulation of little things which create the highest degree of havoc. It is comforting to know that it is not just inexperienced stepfamilies who suffer from this problem. William's story is a salutary lesson.

Tessa and I met when we had both been divorced for some years from our former partners. By coincidence we each had two sons. Mine, however, were grown up while Tessa's were then only seven and nine.

Their father had played virtually no part in their lives, and so when we decided to marry it was a foregone conclusion that the boys would be living with us full-time – in other words, if I wanted Tessa I had to accept I was getting a package deal. That was fine with me – I knew about boys. In fact, I was rather looking forward to being a stepfather.

Right from the beginning I was surprised at how undisciplined they were. Tessa is an extremely successful financial advisor, very high-powered really – a decisive, intelligent woman, and I had imagined she'd stand no nonsense from her children. In fact the reverse is true; they walk all over her.

I was happy to put up with most things – recognising it wasn't supposed to be an easy time for any of us – but the one thing I couldn't stand was their apparent inability to go to bed at a decent hour. In my view children of their age, particularly during termtime, should be in bed by nine o'clock at the very latest. But Tessa let them stay up all evening, and we all went to bed at the same time.

They are intelligent boys but very hyper-active, and the result was that Tessa and I had absolutely no time to ourselves. By the time we crawled into bed we'd absolutely had it for the day.

I began by trying to be reasonable, and asked her whether she couldn't introduce a little discipline about bedtime. I offered to help, to be the scapegoat, but she wouldn't hear of it. She said they didn't need any more sleep, and that in any event it was important that we had time together as a family. When I pointed out that we also needed time together as a couple, she got tearful and said that obviously I didn't like her sons. It was a hopeless situation.

To make matters worse, the more I thought about it the

more I realised what a ludicrous situation it was. One of the reasons the boys irritated me so much at night was that they were over-tired and overwrought and therefore behaved badly. They needed to be in bed, but could I get Tessa to see this? No way.

I began coming home late, finding excuses to finish off a bit of extra work here and there. I found myself popping into the local on the way home for a quick one. Then it became two and three – anything really, to stay out of the house while those boys were up. My relationship with Tessa deteriorated, and then one evening in the pub I met an old girlfriend. We went back to her place, and one thing led to another and we began meeting regularly. I'm not proud of any of this, but I just couldn't stand things at home.

It all ended unhappily. Needless to say, Tessa and I split up and she's back on her own with the boys now. I honestly don't think she's suited to being a mother, a working woman and a wife – I think it's all to much. There are too many demands on her time, so that she can't see the wood for the trees. If I said to people that my marriage broke up because my stepsons didn't go to bed at a reasonable time, they'd think I was joking or mad. The fact is that's what broke up our marriage.

Whether William would have ended up at the pub in any event, we'll never know. But certainly the boys appear to have driven him out of the house at night, and one can understand his point of view. Maybe, though, he should have tried harder, introduced some sort of compromise – I'll play Monopoly with you instead of reading the paper, provided you're in bed by half-past nine,' that sort of thing. Perhaps this is not how he wanted to spend his evening, but becoming a stepparent does require some sacrifices.

Airing problems

So, what can be done to improve the situation if you find that a stepchild's behaviour, or indeed yor partner's behaviour, is driving you potty – where do you begin?

One solution, of course, is simply to wait for the children to grow up – but by then you might well be registered insane. The best reliever of tension is to talk out the problem.

In our family we used to have a fortnightly meeting, a sort of forum in which all the family took part and at which all sorts of problems were aired. This does not mean a heavy session – they were usually quite light-hearted get-togethers. What they did was to provide a framework in which it was acceptable to talk about anything connected with the family and relationships – or, indeed, anything else which was causing concern. And I have to say it worked well.

If you don't set up these 'meetings', things tend to drift. Inevitably parents and step-parents put off confrontation, which in turn allows the problem to escalate and become more serious. Having a regular session takes the drama out of the situation, too. The first talk may be a bit tense and even embarrassing but if you persevere you will find that the sessions become easier. I suppose it's rather like group therapy.

Any child from seven upwards could take part in such a discussion, although if your family covers a large agespan – which, of course, stepfamilies often do – it is possible that you might need one for younger children and another for the older ones. Do make sure that, in your effort to air your own grievances, you allow and encourage your children to do the same. If this is to be a proper forum, then all members are free to express their views and must expect to have their problems and desires taken seriously.

Similarly, don't let the meetings degenerate into one long moan. Use the forum as an opportunity to praise a child for a particular achievement or an overall change of attitude. Be prepared to admit when you may have been at fault – made the wrong decision, over-reacted or whatever. Children are deeply appreciative of parents who are prepared to apologise when they have done something wrong. It also creates an excellent example.

Carol's story is encouraging:

I can't pretend that our family life is a bed of roses, but it's certainly a lot better than it was. Matthew and I knew we were in for a rough time when we got married. He has two boys, sixteen and eighteen, and I have a boy and a girl of fifteen and eleven – a recipe for disaster.

The trouble was that, when we first got together, everything was so chaotic that there was no real time for anybody to discuss anything. We were just existing, getting huge meals on the table on time, getting everybody off to school and various after-school activities, mountains of washing. And we live in the country, so we're endlessly having to ferry the kids about. Fred, Matthew's eldest son, is old enough to drive, but he's at technical college and, to be honest, we can't afford to buy him a car at the moment.

With all this going on, it seemed to me that I never had any time for the children and really I had no idea what they were thinking or feeling about anything. Matthew and I both work – we have to, to support the kids.

I was moaning about it one night and Matthew came up with the idea that perhaps we should have a weekly family meeting. I said the children would hate it, but in fact when we asked them they thought it was a good idea. We decided to make it Wednesdays, which was the one evening everyone was normally around, and right from the beginning we told everybody it was a priority and they had to be there. It would only last half an hour, but attendance was expected.

It was absolutely mind-boggling the things we found out about the children – how they felt about us and themselves. After our first meeting, both Matthew and I were simply gobsmacked. They all had such strong views, even the eleven-year-old, and were fairly critical about some of the things we did. I must say in most respects they were right, and they even slung us a few compliments as well!

As the weeks went by, I honestly think we all began to enjoy our meetings. They became an extension of our evening meal. Then Matthew started bringing home a bottle of wine to turn it into something of an occasion.

I can honestly say, for our family, it was a complete turning-point. It gave us all an opportunity to understand each other's problems and difficulties. Matthew and I were completely frank in telling the children how we felt, and I think it helps sometimes for children to see that their parents are just are vulnerable as they are. It's wrong, particularly with children of our age, to continue to set oneself up as some sort of God-like figure who knows the answer to everything. Frankly, it's been the making of us.

So fix up your meetings, and don't consider it as something you will only do if you strike major problems. It is a good idea anyway to have a formal structure in which you all communicate, particularly while you are learning to be a family. It may be that you all get so good at living and loving together that you abandon the talks. Fair enough, they will have served their purpose – but make sure in the meantime that they always receive top priority. We never allowed our older children to miss one, even if they had a heavy date, but similarly we had to make sure that we were back from work – it's one rule for everyone.

Outside help

If the relationship has broken down to the point where talking does no good, consider seeking help from one of the organisations listed on page 138. The glorious thing about talking through your problems to an outsider is that you will immediately discover that you are not alone and that there is nothing wrong with *you*. What you are experiencing has been experienced by many, many families before you. So don't be afraid to lift the telephone and dial a help-line. If you value your marriage, if you want a good relationship with your stepchildren, don't be afraid to try anything.

Donna's desperation saved her stepfamily from heart-break:

Things between Neil and me had never been good since we married, what with the stress of our jobs and of trying to make our family work – two of mine and one of his. We fought all the time, the children fought – it was just ghastly. We seemed to be sinking further and further into an abyss and I could see no way out.

At one point I suggested to Neil that perhaps we should consider seeking some professional help. He was appalled at the idea, saying it was nobody's business but our own and he wasn't going to have do-gooders interfering. So that was that – we battled on. I couldn't bear the thought of another divorce – I thought my children had been through enough, not to mention myself. And yet, equally, I knew we couldn't go on as we were.

One evening, just before Christmas, we went round to a neighbour's party. It is a regular 'do' each year and they ask the entire neighbourhood, including our local vicar, with whom I had a nodding acquaintance, although I have to admit we are not regular churchgoers.

Neil and I had quite a bit to drink, I suppose because of all the tension at home and because we didn't have to drive. I found myself talking to the vicar, who was very easy and approachable and suggested I called him Mark – I remember saying what a very biblical name it was. I must have been very drunk!

He started asking me about our family and I was so embarrassed. I began giving him the usual platitudes, and suddenly I was crying. He seemed to understand immediately and led me off to our host's study. It all poured out – everything. I even told him how our sex life had become non-existent – I can't believe it now.

He listened very carefully and then told me to sit there while he replenished my drink. When he came back he had Neil with him. I thought Neil would be furious, but instead he seemed to be putty in Mark's hands. He asked Neil to tell him his side of the story, and Neil came out with a lot of stuff I didn't even know about – like how he felt I favoured my children over his, how I was a completely different person when the children were around, so tense and irritable. I hardly recognized myself.

At the end of it all, Mark said there was one thing which was clear and certain in all the mess – we still loved each other, and that to lose everything we had would be an appalling waste. He suggested that we should go to RELATE – he knew a counsellor there and, if we liked, he would have a word in advance.

Much to my astonishment, Neil agreed. We left the party and walked home. That night we made love for the first time in weeks. I thought in the morning Neil would say we didn't need help, but when I tentatively suggested ringing RELATE he agreed.

Now, six months later, we are on the right track. The children are more settled and so are we. I'm not saying all our problems are over, but at least now we discuss them, both with one another and with our counsellor. We're going to make it, we both feel that. I'm expecting a baby in the autumn. We thought we'd ask Mark to be its godfather.

So talking amongst yourselves, to your friends, to professional counsellors, to self-help groups, will all relieve the tensions, keep the problems in proportion and help you recognise you are not alone.

Tackling problems before they arise

The most successful 'cure' is to tackle the problem before it arises – to discover the art of administering preventative medicine. One of the reasons that so many stepfamilies break down is because of confusion, because nobody's role is clear and no one knows what is happening next – there is no structure, no rules and therefore no security.

Right from the very first day you begin living together as a family, organise your lives in such a way that everyone knows what is going on. You must develop an agenda so that everyone knows what is expected of them. All arrangements connected with visits to other parents, where weekends and holidays are to be spent, who is attending speech days, sports days or plays, need to be ironed out well in advance.

The headmaster of a boys' public school told me that,

just before the end of term, an enormous number of pupils do not know where they are going to spend the holidays. He says this uncertainty, more than anything else, upsets the boys. Not only can they not plan and envisage their much-needed holidays, but the fact that the arrangements have not yet been made demonstrates an appalling lack of care on the part of the parents. It suggests that their sons' holidays are of no importance to them – that they are something that can be organised at the last minute, like a trip to the supermarket. Of all the problems he has to face in the running of a big school, he considers this the most heartbreaking.

You don't want to run your family like a military operation, and of course there must always be room for spontaneous fun and sudden changes of plan which turn a routine day into a party day. But children like to know what is going on and what will happen next.

Let's say there is a school concert planned. You are busy, but she wants to know who is going to come to the concert. Can her father take time off work? Will you come? Should she ring her mother and ask her? Miraculously, could you all come or would that be embarrassing? She needs to know fast what the arrangements are.

It may seem trivial to you, but there are so many important things at stake for her and, above all, she does not want to be let down in front of her peers. They will already know she is part of a broken family and she wants to demonstrate that, despite it, her parents and her stepmother really care about her. She has been practising her violin for weeks, and her interest in music may have been a solace to her in the last few difficult months or years. Perhaps you have only just got together as a family, so she doesn't know what to expect. She is nervous and uncertain: she cannot take anything for granted any longer because the world she knew has been destroyed. So 'Don't worry, one of us will come,' is no good. You need to get it sorted out immediately.

What applies to a school concert applies to every detail of your stepchildren's life. It is not fair, when other children at school are talking about Christmas plans, for your stepchild not to be able to join in because he does not know whether he will be spending Christmas with Mummy, Mummy's boyfriend's family, Daddy and his new wife, or the grandparents. It makes him different, it makes him insecure.

So get organised, and stay that way. If you do, you may well find that much of the strife and tension which are considered such a normal part of the average stepfamily simply will not apply to yours.

9

The Flashpoints

Tragically, the times when a family should be at its most joyous are, so far as the stepfamily is concerned, usually the most stressful. These times are family celebrations – Christmas, birthdays, holidays, weddings, christenings. Mention Christmas, and both natural parents are likely to start ranting and raving about their rights as to where their children should be, with no apparent concern for what the children might want.

Most of us have fond memories of childhood birthdays – of friends and loving family, of a party and presents, jellies, party games, of being the centre of attention – of being special. This is every child's right, and yet all too often the day that is supposed to be the celebration of their very existence is just another excuse for their parents to have an argument. I know of several children who dread their own birthdays.

Maria is now in her forties but she is still haunted by her school holidays:

My father and mother split up when my brother and I were about six and eight. My mother ran off with a Frenchman and set up home with him in Paris. My father, a fairly large landowner in Northamptonshire, gained custody of us, and then packed us both off to boarding school.

It was obviously a very unhappy time for us, but it was made so much worse by my parents wrangling over the holidays. My mother thought we should spend them with her and my father thought we should spend them with him. We never knew what was happening. Sometimes, to resolve their disputes, my brother would go to one and I to the other, which we hated – we so much preferred to be together, to give each other moral support.

In retrospect, I don't think either of them particularly wanted us. My father didn't know how to handle us at all and left us to the servants, and my mother's smart Paris apartment and her sophisticated Parisian boyfriend did not create the right environment for two children raised in the country. We embarrassed them, and they embarrassed us.

When everybody else at school was looking forward to the holidays, we dreaded them. School was our only real source of security, the only place where we could be relaxed and be ourselves. I've never had children, and I'm sure it's because I can't bear the thought of hurting them as my parents hurt us.

This chapter will help you consider family celebrations – particularly those related specifically to the child – from the child's point of view, and then to adjust your thinking accordingly.

Christmas

This is supposed to be a time for children. Any family that has not enjoyed the company of children for some years will speak of the very special joy that comes from suddenly having, say, grandchildren joining the family group. Children turn Christmas into a magical time. Around the world there will be many children who feel they are spending their Christmas Day in a place in which they do not want to be, and sharing the celebrations with the wrong person. This situation will most likely have been caused by the insensitivity of their parents and step-parents.

It is certainly natural for parents to want to spend all or part of the Christmas festivities with their child. There are even grounds for saying that the non-custodial parents, who see much less of their children than their former partners, should be given access over Christmas. Against this argument is the fact that most children would like to spend Christmas in their own home – waking up in their own bed on Christmas morning to find their bulging stockings, telephoning or visiting their school friends, going to the local church where there are familiar faces in the congregation, spending the day surrounded by people whom they know and love best. But this view is sadly often neglected.

Many separated couples congratulate themselves on the fairness with which they handle Christmas. The children go to one parent one year and the other the next. But is this what children really want? If asked, particularly while they are young, you will almost certainly find that a child wants to spend Christmas in the same place every year. To maximise their security and enjoyment they want to build up a series of rituals which form a framework for the day. Children are very conformist and conventional. They have an idealistic view of how things should be, and they want it acted out. It should also be their right to have a relaxed day, and how can this possibly happen if they have Christmas lunch with Mummy and Christmas dinner with Daddy?

Of course Christmas does not have to evolve exclusively around the children. Most parents and step-parents will have worked very hard throughout the year to make the celebration possible and they, too, have earned a little respite from life's daily drag. Children should also be encouraged to have a sense of responsibility for other people's happiness; just because they want to do something, it does not necessarily make it right or desirable for everyone else – a lesson, incidentally, which many parents could well benefit from. Listen to the story told by nineteen-year-old Steven:

> My parents divorced when I was eight and both remarried quite quickly. I have always lived with my Mum and get on well with my stepdad – he's a nice bloke. I am not so keen on my father's wife, but she's OK.
>
> Because my parents still live in the same town, it has been possible to see plenty of my father, although I don't live with him. So things should have been pretty easy really – and I suppose they have in most respects, looking back on it.

123

The stumbling block, though, was always Christmas, and to a lesser extent my birthday. Every year, my Dad and my Mum both thought I should spend it with them. On my birthday I simply divided the day between them, because it always fell in the school holidays. However, things were much more complicated at Christmas. They began arguing in about November, and as a kid I can remember, when all my school friends were really looking forward to Christmas, all I could think about was the rows and the unpleasantness.

When I was fifteen I started a Saturday job at a local fish and chip shop, and at sixteen they took me on in the evenings sometimes as well. By the time Christmas came round when I was seventeen I had quite a bit of money saved, so with a couple of friends I booked a skiing holiday. I didn't tell either of my parents I was going until twenty-four hours before I left. They both went mad and said I couldn't go.

Funnily enough, the only person who stuck up for me was my stepmother. She said she could understand exactly why I didn't want another family Christmas, so they let me go. I have been skiing on both Christmasses since – it's quite a laugh, although it does feel a bit odd being away from your family. Still, it solves the problem. I'm never going to have Christmas at home again, that's for sure.

The pre-Christmas hype in schools, shops and the media is considerable. Nativity plays and carol concerts at school are only the end result – before that there are weeks of rehearsals, card and decorations making and general anticipation. We are all, including very small children, under huge pressure to have a lovely time at Christmas. For children who know they are going to be the centre of a storm, it must be all the more galling to feel that everyone else's Christmas is going to be wonderful – even though, of course, the reality is often different.

So the best thing is to try and sort out arrangements that reflect the child's genuine wishes, with as little animosity as possible, and to do so well in advance. As mentioned in Chapter 8, it can be very upsetting for children not to know what is going to happen to them over an important event like Christmas. Again, their peers will be asking about their plans and they need to know, well in advance, particularly if it is some new arrangement which requires a degree of adjustment.

Birthdays

Let's imagine for a moment that you are seven years old and it is your birthday. How would you like to spend it? I think there is little doubt that almost every child would like to spend his or her birthday at home, celebrating with a group of their very best friends, at a conventional birthday tea party. Ask the same child the same question at twelve and you might find that he or she would like to go to the cinema, swimming, roller-skating or to a theme park, but again with a group of friends.

This, then, is the key to birthdays: most children want to be with their peer group. They want to have a good time and, while we parents might kid ourselves that we can be quite fun and youthful, the fact is that we have no idea how to party like a seven-year-old. There is also his image to consider. If his best friend had a super party with a magic-man, then he wants the same. If his friend had a birthday cake which looked like Thomas the Tank Engine, when he wants one which looks like James or Henry or another of Reverend Awdrey's creations – and why not?

As a step-parent or parent, this should be your main aim. If both natural parents live close by, it is quite possible that the child's main birthday treat can take place in either house. However, if the non-custodial parent lives some distance away, then he or she should not interfere with the child's main birthday celebration – unless, of course, relations are so good that you can visit the other natural parent's home without embarrassment. So if you find yourself the non-custodial step-parent, try and encourage your partner to stand back from the child's main celebration and allow him to spend it in a conventional way, probably with his peers. That does not mean that the non-custodial parent should not celebrate his child's birthday at all. On the next access visit, a second celebration will make the child feel he has two birthdays – that he is special twice over.

Parents' birthdays need to be considered, too. When the parents of a child are happily married to one another, they naturally help their child to choose, and often pay for, a gift for the other parent when their birthday comes round, and indeed at Christmas. This aspect is very often overlooked once the parents are divorced, and it can be a source of great upset for a child. If Mummy and Daddy are always at loggerheads and do not have a good word to say about one another, how can you ask one to help buy a present for the other? Equally, they may feel that the step-parent will not understand.

Just because parents split up and cease to love one another, there is no reason why the children of their marriage should not continue to love both parents. Given this, it is natural that the children will want to give their parents a gift, and only right that they should be encouraged to do so. This may particularly apply to the parent with whom the children are not living. They may well feel guilty about seeing so little of their parent, although it is not their fault, and would like to find some means of expressing the fact that they still love, care and think about their parent, even though circumstances keep them apart. As a step-parent, make sure you are aware of the birthdays of all the people who are important in your stepchildren's lives – grandparents, godparents, aunts, cousins – and help them in any way you can. Gwen's story concerns a wedding rather than a birthday but it still makes the point:

My daughter, Tina, divorced when Alec, her son, was six. She met Hugh the following year and they decided to marry, shortly before Alec's eighth birthday. I have always been very close to my grandson, because Tina started working again shortly after his first birthday and I looked after him for her until he started school.

I felt sure that Hugh was an ideal husband for Tina – far more satisfactory than Alec's father had been. I also thought he would make Alec a wonderful stepfather, so I was surprised when Tina telephoned me to say that she was very worried about Alec – he seemed to be very unhappy and on edge. With the wedding only days away, she could only imagine that this was troubling him and was starting to wonder whether she had done the right thing. When she tried to talk to him he had completely clammed up on her, so she asked if I could have a quiet word with him and see if I could make any progress.

I collected Alec from school the following day and he came back to tea with me. Over his favourite chocolate cake, I asked him if there was anything wrong. To start with he said no, and then he admitted that there was. I asked him if he was happy about his Mummy marrying Hugh and he said yes, he was, but he had a problem he couldn't tell Mummy. By this time I was getting very anxious, as you can imagine.

Over a refill of tea and another slice of cake, the story tumbled out. He wanted to buy Mummy and Hugh a wedding present. Wedding presents had been flooding into their house for some days and he suddenly realised that this was something people did. He loved his Mummy very much, he said, and was very glad she was marrying Hugh, but he hadn't enough money – only twenty-seven pence – and there didn't seem to be much he could buy for that.

The relief was so enormous and his sentiment so touching I have to admit to having a bit of a cry. When we had mopped each other up, Alec and I went off on a shopping spree and went a bit mad. We bought a lovely print for Hugh and Tina collectively, and then a jumper for Tina and a shirt for Hugh as individual presents as well. Alec was very pleased – it was as if the troubles of the world had fallen off his shoulders.

I could have kicked myself for being so insensitive – I should have realised the situation myself and saved him all this heartache. Tina felt exactly the same when I told her the problem. We both felt we had failed him.

The problems of the older 'child'

The divorce of their parents can prove very upsetting for adult children. When they have established a life of their own, and perhaps even have a family of their own, you would not think that their parents' relationship breaking down would cause too much grief. In fact, the reverse is often true.

By definition, the breakdown of a marriage between the parents of adult children takes place after many years of being together. Something that the children have always taken for granted, which has formed the backbone of their life, disintegrates. It has the effect of making them question everything – their own lives, perhaps their own marriages. Suddenly nothing is safe and secure any more, and they begin to recognise their own vulnerability.

All this may seem rather selfish. If two middle-aged or elderly people decided to change their lives, then how their adult children feel should be of no consequence – or should it? Isabel made a clear choice.

It may seem rather an eccentric decision, but Freddy and I agreed to part when he retired. We'd always been very different – I suppose that's what attracted us to one another in the first place. We married very young, then had four children very quickly, and for years we did not really have to confront the issue of whether we got along as two people. Freddy had his work; I had the children. I expect he had affairs, I don't know, but the interesting thing is I could never really have cared.

It was only when the children left home and Freddy, with retirement looming, needed to work less hard that we were thrown into one another's company more often. We found we were complete strangers – not only strangers, but with no particular desire to get to know one another better again. Of course we have a lot of shared past – forty years of marriage, four lovely children, grandchildren – but the differences are greater than ever.

Freddy is a great amateur yachtsman. His idea of retirement

is to go and live down somewhere on the Solent and have a boat. I can't think of anything I would like to do less. My life is here in London, with my friends. I'm a city person, always have been, and as for boats, I can't bear them.

So we took what we believed was a very sensible and adult decision. Neither of us have any intention of every marrying again, so there's no question of us divorcing – why make the lawyers fat? We just agreed to part. Freddy has bought a cottage down in the New Forest. I've retained the house here, which is big enough for the children to come and stay. And we've agreed, of course, that we will meet on special family occasions unless either of us has something better to do.

You would think that would be the end of the story, but not a bit of it. The children were absolutely up in arms, appalled at our decision, telling us that we must be out of our minds, that we would be lonely and miserable, that it would never work. To start with, both Freddy and I were rather alarmed by this outcry. Perhaps they were right. But the more we thought about it the more we came to the conclusion that what they were really being was selfish. They didn't like the concept of having their parents in two separate places. It's ludicrous to say that we would be lonely – we have led separate lives all these years anyway. Freddy has his sailing cronies, I have my lifelong friends – and besides, if we really miss each other we can always meet, though I doubt we will very often. I just don't understand the children at all.

As a parent or step-parent you need to appreciate that, even though the children may be grown up, you still have the ability to hurt them very badly indeed. A bride's wedding day can be ruined by trying to work out whether her father or her stepfather should walk her up the aisle. A young mother's first anxious weeks with her new baby can be made even more stressful by the grandparents trying to outdo each other. Just bear in mind that there is a child in all of us. We all need reassurance, praise and support, particularly at life's milestones. If you are a step-parent of older children, remember that they still need parental support from time to time. Do what you can to make it easier for everyone.

Holidays

These occasions are perfect for a non-custodial parent to make his or her mark. A holiday implies a change, hopefully a stimulating and enjoyable change from day-to-day activity – a different scene, a different way of life. Whereas for traditional celebrations a child may prefer to be in his main home, holidays can take place anywhere, and up to a point with anyone – and still conform to his idea of what is normal. It is usually better for non-custodial parents to see their children for a reasonable length of time rather than weekend or Sunday access visits which tend to be unsettling. Over a week or two parent and child can really get to know one another again properly, in an unstressed situation. If it is a true holiday and the parent is off work, the amount of prime time available to the child is probably equivalent to months or even years of brief access meetings.

However much the custodial parent loves his or her child, a break is never a bad thing. If the custodial parent has married again, a break provides an opportunity for parent and step-parent to be on their own for a while; this is good for the family as a whole as well as for the couple.

Custodial parents have a tendency to be wary and frightened of prolonged access visits to the former partner, in case they lose the affection of their child. As a step-parent you could help your partner to overcome this. Nothing can be more rewarding for all members of the family than if the child can have a happy holiday with the parent he sees least often. He will probably return a happier and easier child than when he left. If the holiday has not been a huge success, on the other hand, he does not need to repeat it – if nothing else, it will have made him appreciate home comforts!

Holidays with an already warring stepfamily can be

fraught. If as a family you are not getting on very well at home, being thrown into each other's company twenty-four hours a day can be an absolute disaster. Against this, of course, is the point made earlier. When you go away from home, strangers meeting you assume you are a normal family and this can prove quite help-ful – balm to the soul, perhaps even drawing you together as it did my own family:

> When Lucy was still quite young, eight or nine, she and I and Alan went on an extended trip to Canada and the USA to visit various relations. We had all sorts of adventures, criss-crossing the country and ending up in Texas visiting Lucy's half-brother and my No.2 stepson. Alan and I had not been married long, and without a doubt this holiday threw the three of us together. We were like a small band of gypsies, travelling from home to home meeting new sets of people. All these years later we still talk about the trip – it was special, a very important part of the bonding process.

So whatever the circumstances of your family holiday, try to remember that holidays are supposed to be fun and a time for relaxation, perhaps away from the drudgery of daily life, when closer relationships can be formed and improved upon.

Drama

Illness, injury or death are the obvious dramas of life. So, too, are an unwanted pregnancy, majory truancy, or a problem with drink or drugs or the police. You would think that when their child is in trouble, perhaps even in a life-threatening situation, parents would bury the hatchet and think only of the child's wellbeing. But this is not always so, as Sue explains:

> Bobby had been cycling round to his friend's house for months, ever since his eighth birthday when we bought his new bicycle. Harry and I were quite happy about it – there was a cycle path all the way and he only had to cross one road, a

minor one. We always rang his friend's Mum before he left, so that she could ring us if he didn't turn up – the ride only took ten minutes.

On that Saturday, Bobby left to go round to his friend's after lunch. His friend's Mum rang about twenty minutes later to say he hadn't arrived and almost at the same moment there was a policeman at the door. I knew, of course. He was in Intensive Care. Apparently a driver had just left the pub and mounted the pavement. Bobby didn't stand a chance.

When Tom, my ex-husband (Bobby's father) arrived, he started straightaway – telling me I was an irresponsible parent, that I should never have let Bobby out of my sight, that he was going to die and it was my fault. I'll never forget it, sitting there, waiting to hear if my son was alive or dead while his father hurled this abuse at me. Bobby lived – he had weeks in hospital, but he was a brave little boy and now he's as right as rain. But I'll never speak to his father again – never.

Tragedies can bring people together, but equally, shock can make them react in a strange way. Maybe Tom is not by nature vindictive but was simply reacting to the horror of the situation in the only way he could. That Sue is not in a position to give him the benefit of the doubt is not entirely surprising, but refusing to speak to Tom again is in the long term going to hurt Bobby most.

All too often when something goes wrong with their child, the natural parent's first reaction is to start apportioning blame – most usually the non-custodial parent accusing the custodial parent of causing the problem in the first place. In an otherwise 'normal' family, parents facing the dilemma of their fourteen-year-old daughter becoming pregnant would naturally look inwards and see where they themselves might have gone wrong. In a happy marriage they would assume the blame collectively. Although their self-searching would be unlikely to have any practical benefit, at least it would not be destructive.

In the same circumstances but where the girl's parents

were divorced, the father would probably blame the mother for not looking after her better and the mother would blame the father for setting her a bad example. All this would achieve is to add to the already considerable burden of pressure and pain from which the child was suffering. As in so many instances throughout this book, the best role for the step-parent is to try and diffuse, to try and draw the natural parent's mind away from whose fault it is, to looking at what best can be done for the benefit of the child.

Conclusion

I hope that throughout this book I have been able to convey one clear message – that step-parenthood should be a very positive thing. Step-parents have a great deal to offer the children who are permanently, or occasionally, in their care. They are not parents and they are not friends, they are something in between, and in an odd way perhaps all the more valuable for that. They stand for authority but not in an emotionally charged, over-protective way. They are caring by-standers – or they should be.

Step-parents can be of enormous benefit not only to children but also to the natural parents. So often step-parents can see things far more clearly because they are not directly involved; and while, of course, it is danger-ous to interfere too much, their help in seeing the wood for the trees can prove invaluable. Being a step-parent is not a bed of roses, but it need not be a bed of nails either.

A recurring theme with step-parents I have spoken to is their feeling of inadequacy, particularly in the early days of the relationship with their stepchildren. Many said how ill-equipped they felt at suddenly finding themselves pushed into the role of parent, and in retro-spect they felt that it was their inexperience that caused many of the problems between themselves and their stepchildren. It is difficult. Nature gives us nine months to become acclimatised to the idea of parenthood, and even doles out appropriate hormones to the mother to help her cope. Step-parenthood is not only thrust upon you, but you have the disadvantage of having to make a relationship against the backdrop of an established one with their natural parent.

In retrospect, it appears that many step-parents wish

they had been more understanding towards their stepchildren. Often it is not until they have become parents themselves that they fully appreciate the problems of their stepchildren and see how they could have dealt with them more kindly. It is easy to take advantage of children because of their unequal status. Try to imagine that the child in your care is an adult; then ask yourself whether your behaviour towards him is acceptable. Is his view given enough consideration? Are you spending enough time listening to his troubles and taking an interest in his life? Is he being used as a pawn in the manipulating game that goes on between his parents? If so, what can you do to help?

This advice, of course, is all very well if you genuinely like your stepchildren and want to learn to love them, but what happens if you do not like them at all? What do you do if you genuinely feel that your relationship with them has no future, that you are locked into a situation from which you cannot escape?

Not surprisingly, some step-parents cannot stand their stepchildren, and vice versa. Whether it stems from a direct clash of personalities or simply the circumstances of their lives together hardly matters. The problem is that, if the relationship does not gel, the strain for everyone is immense. But it is still desperately important that you try to do the right thing, not just on moral grounds but because the situation may not be so black in the long term.

It may be that you are no good at dealing with small children or that you are very young yourself and need to grow up a bit before you can handle step-parenthood. Maybe the relationship with your new partner is sapping all your emotional energy. Maybe your job is so demanding you have little time for anything else – nor, indeed, the inclination. Do not despair, for at some stage in the child's life you may come into your own. Adolescence, for example, is always regarded as a fraught time, but a great many adults cannot communicate with small children and yet thoroughly enjoy dealing with adolescents. The important thing is never to write off the relationship with your stepchild, however awful things may seem; they will change, and almost always for the better. If right from the beginning you behave in a way which you feel is in the child's best interest, no matter what provocation you may receive, ultimately you stand a very good chance of forming a worthwhile bond.

Think for a moment of the situation we all experience with long friendships. At various stages during your life you will rarely see your friend because for some reason you have little in common. At other times you meet practically every day and get to know every last detail of each other's lives. The circumstances that create this situation are usually practical – your children go to the same playgroup or nursery school, you travel on the same commuter train, you both share a passion for golf. In other words it is not simply friendship that binds people together but circumstances, and so it will be in your relationship with your stepchildren.

The circumstances in which you first become a step-parent may not be conducive to the establishment of a relationship. Perhaps you see the child infrequently or always in a very strained atmosphere. Time, though, may change this – when the child changes schools it might become practical for you to drop him off on your way to work. Suddenly you are thrown together for twenty minutes in the car every morning, and in the inevitable traffic queue you start to talk. By the end of the first term you may have a completely different relationship. It is so often the apparently insignificant things which cause the trouble, but they can also form the bond.

I can honestly say that the person I am today is in many respects due to my stepsons – they helped me grow up, helped me in so many subtle ways towards a better understanding of people and their problems. If you keep your expectations low, the benefits you may derive from being a step-parent can be tremendous.

Whatever the problems, as the years go by they do become easier to cope with as you and your stepchildren learn to live together. Being a parent – natural, step, adoptive, foster – can be a wonderful experience. Like everything else in life, it's what you make of it.

Useful Names and Addresses

British Agencies for Adoption and Fostering: 11 Southwark Street, London SE1 1RQ; tel. 071-407 8800; 40 Shandwick Place, Edinburgh, EH2 4RT; tel. 031-225 9285.

Catholic Marriage Advisory Council: Clitherow House, 15 Lansdowne Road, London W11 3AJ; tel. 071-727 0141 (centres in all major towns).

Child and Family Guidance Centres (or Child Guidance Clinics): check local phone book or ask CAB.

Citizens' Advice Bureau (CAB): check local phone book.

Cruse (National Organisation for the Widowed and their Children): Cruse House, 126 Sheen Road, Richmond, Surrey TW9 1UR; tel. 081 940 4818.

Divorce Conciliation and Advisory Service (help for divorcing couples): 38 Ebury Street, London SW1W 0LU; tel. 071-730 2422.

Families Need Fathers (help for divorced fathers): B.M. Families, London WC1N 3XX; tel. 071-852 7123.

Gingerbread: 35 Wellington Street, London WC2; tel. 071-240 0953.

Jewish Marriage Council: 23 Ravenshurst Avenue, London NW4 4EL; tel. 081-203 6311.

National Council for One Parent Families: 255 Kentish Town Road, London NW5 2LX; tel. 071-237 1361.

National Stepfamily Association: 72 Willesden Lane, London NW6 7TA; tel. 071 372 0844.

National Family Conciliation Council: 34 Milton Road, Swindon, SN1 5JA; tel. 0793 514055.

Northern Ireland Marriage Guidance Council: 76 Dublin Road, Belfast BT2 7HP; tel. 0232 323454.

Parentline: Rayfa House, 57 Hart Road, South Benfleet, Essex; tel. 0268 757077

Relate: check local phone book or ask CAB.

Scottish Catholic Marriage Guidance Council: 18 Park Circus, Glasgow, G3 6BE; tel. 041-332 4914.

Scottish Marriage Guidance Council: 26 Frederick Street, Edinburgh, EH2 2JR; tel. 031-255 5006.

Scottish Council for Single Parents: 13 Gayfield Square, Edinburgh, EH1 3NX; tel. 031-566 3899.

Samaritans: head office 17 Uxbridge Road, Slough, Berks, SL1 1SN, tel. 0753 32713/4. For local offices check local phone book or ask CAB.

Solicitors' Family Law Association: 154 Fleet Street, London, EC4A 2HX.

Women's Aid Federation Ltd (help for battered wives): PO Box 391, Bristol, BS99 7WS; tel. 0272 428368.

Scottish Women's Aid: tel. 031-225 8011.

Welsh Women's Aid: tel. 0222 390874.

Northern Ireland Women's Aid: tel. 0232 249041.

Index

INDEX

If you have enjoyed

Loving Other People's Children

you may also be interested in the following Vermilion titles

The Relate Guide To Better Relationships
by Sarah Litvinoff (£6.99)

The Relate Guide To Sex in Loving Relationships
by Sarah Litvinoff (£6.99)

You and Your Adolescent
by Laurence Steinberg, Ph.D., and Ann Levine (£9.99)

To obtain your copy, simply telephone Murlyn Services on

0279 427203

Your copy will be dispatched to you without delay, postage and packing free. You may pay by cheque/postal order/VISA and should allow 28 days for delivery.